The Authors

Jonny Zucker is a qualified primary school teacher by day and a stand-up comic by night. He currently teaches in the London Borough of Ealing. His favourite teacher was Mr. Leyton who was a black belt at karate and coached the school football team to play a 2-3-5 formation.

David Parker is a qualified primary school teacher. He is currently working on educational research projects at King's College, London. His favourite teacher was Miss. Lomas, who wore a bright blue feather in her hair whenever she took the class for P.E.

A Class Act

Jonny Zucker & David Parker

SAPPHIRE PUBLISHERS LIMITED

First Edition 1999

Published by
Sapphire Publishers Ltd
P O BOX 22715
London N22 7WH

© 1999 Jonny Zucker and David Parker

All rights reserved. No part of this publication may be reproduced, stored in a retrieval system, or transmitted, in any form or by any means, electronic, mechanical, photocopying, recording or otherwise, without the prior permission in writing of Sapphire Publishers Ltd.

A CIP catalogue record for this book is available from the British Library.

ISBN 0-9535432-0-X

Typeset and Graphics by Sophie Lansman
studio.design@dial.pipex.com

Cover Artwork by David Leach
davidaleach@cwcom.net

Printed and bound in Great Britain by
The Jensen Press Limited London N5

For Fiona and Dushani

Acknowledgements

Massive thanks to Sophie Lansman for her layout skills, graphics, time and patience; David Leach for his superb work on the cover and flexibility; Paul Fenton and everyone at Jensen Press for all of their brilliant work and effort; James Libson and Sam Clarke for advice and assistance.

Thanks also to all of the following who have helped us through discussions, suggestions and staff meetings: Our families, Wendy Dixon and all staff, past and present, at West Acton Primary School, Anne Joseph, Alison Goodman, Nick Lansman, Tim Lawrence, Enrica Balestra, Elliot Boyd, Jane Gordon, Robert Lobato, Dalia Lyons, Julia Boley, Mark Elton, Sophie Parry-Williams, Dave Marcus, Sam Turner, Peter Arbeid, Miriam Bindman, Dave Cohen, Paul Glanz, Toby Chislett.

We would also like to thank Tim Brighouse, Christopher Woodhead, Doug McAvoy and Nigel de Gruchy for granting us interviews, and their administrative staffs for helping set these up.

A special thank you to Fiona Starr and Dushani Parker who amongst other things, listened to and offered improvements for each section of *A Class Act* as it was completed, proof-read the text, and encouraged us in all of our endeavours to produce this book.

Contents

Introduction

1. *What shall I do with the remaining 72,500 hours of my working life?*
   Why do people become teachers?

2. *What they should learn and how they should learn it*
   The vacuum-packed year that is teacher training

3. *On remand for good behaviour*
   The teacher's probationary year

4. Interview with Tim Brighouse

5. *Who's in charge here?*
   Teachers and pupils in schools today

6. *Don't call me colleague!*
   How do teachers get on with their fellow professionals?

7. *Captain, you're wanted on the bridge*
   Meet your senior management team

8. Interview with Doug McAvoy

9. *Butchers, bakers, candlestick makers*
   A who's who of non-teaching staff

10. *I don't mean to be a pain but...*
    Parent power and schools

11. *Are you lookin' at me?*
    The misery of inspection week

12. Interview with Chris Woodhead

13. *How to terrorise a small village*
    Taking children on school trips

14. *The pot noodle as a luxury item*
    Teachers and money

15. *Bring back the ducking stool*
    Why teachers are made scapegoats
    for all of society's ills

16. Interview with Nigel de Gruchy

17. *The Great Escape*
    Leave if you must, but don't close the door

18. Conclusion

A Class Act

A Class Act

Introduction

We met for the first time several years ago as we took our places at an unfeasonably small table, in a room of twenty or so adults. We were gathered to partake in a discussion entitled; *How can you best portray the themes from Charlie and the chocolate factory in the form of a classroom wall display?*

We were students on a Postgraduate Certificate of Education course (PGCE) at Roehampton Institute. We were both determined to qualify as teachers, but we were into making some mischief on the journey. On the one hand we accepted that playing dice games in maths sessions was an important pathway into numeracy, but on the other we couldn't stop ourselves from singing *'Luck be a lady tonight'* as we threw a double six. This combination of seriousness and frivolity stayed with us as we left the safety of the teacher-training institution and entered the real world.

In our respective schools we encountered similar experiences. Some of them surreal. Some of them inspiring. Some simply terrifying. In exchanging classroom tales with one another the seed of an idea took root in our minds. As teachers always have stories to tell and concerns to share with one another, why not collect some between the covers of a book?

Our approach was relatively straightforward. We took every aspect we could think of about schools and teaching, and completely tore them apart. Amongst countless other questions we asked ourselves were; Why would anyone want to become a teacher today? Do kids and teachers hate each other? How tense is the atmosphere in a staffroom? Are school trips really a total nightmare? What makes an Ofsted inspector tick? Is it possible to fall in love with someone who specialises in craft techniques?

We wrote *A Class Act* in the 'pamphleteer' spirit, taking our cue from those men and women who condensed their passion, anger and humour into homespun roughly pasted leaflets, and then stood on street corners trying to attract buyers. We considered imitating their marketing approach but rejected it on the grounds of inclement weather.

With the assistance of those helpful souls at directory enquiries, we rang some leading figures in the educational world, and asked if we could interview them for our book. Christopher Woodhead, Tim Brighouse, Doug McAvoy and Nigel de Gruchy all kindly agreed, and we decided that without being too forward, we would ask the questions most teachers would want us to ask them.

A Class Act is not a set work for any course (as yet), and does not come highly recommended by any leading theorists. It will in no way improve your academic

A Class Act

credentials and will not necessarily make you more attractive (although torn up and worn as breeches, it does convey a certain sensuous air).

So go on, make a cup of your favourite brew, sit back in the comfiest chair you can find, and prepare to have all of your beliefs about schools smashed forever.

Jonny Zucker and David Parker - London 1999.

A Class Act

1. *What shall I do with the remaining 75,200 hours of my working life?*

Why do people choose to become teachers?

Let's be honest, who in their right minds would even consider for a nanosecond, the possibility of a career in teaching?

The prospect of putting up with a class of noisy, irresponsible, selfish, grumpy, uncooperative, irrespectful, attitude-laden, greedy, unkind, possibly emotionally unstable, children, all day, is not a pleasant one in any time and space dimension, let alone the one we know as harsh reality. Add to that potentially terrifying mixture, the grief that can be dished out by parents, other teachers, school governors, a malicious press and successive governmental regimes bent on re-inventing the whole profession partly for their own political aims, and you have a job that is about as tasty as food-tester for Cleopatra.

AND YET, sane, respectable people in their thousands, apply each year for teacher-training courses, with a view to actually practising their craft at sometime in the future, in return for a mediocre wage and an endless mountain of books to mark with comments such as *Good effort, but please watch your capital letters.*

AND YES, some do drop out of these courses, and pursue other career paths or life choices, but many more stay with the training and go on to teach.

We did it, and just look at us now. Sitting under the clock at Waterloo station at ten a.m on a Tuesday morning, with a bottle of whiskey to share and last week's crossword from *Railway World* to complete. But we've been there, seen it, had it large on the educational scene, linked organically by set-squares and endless reams of lined scrap paper. But don't pity us, celebrate with us, and raise a glass to all of those folk who are bold enough to contemplate setting that first timid step on the road to teaching.

Having asked ourselves the question time and time again, why does anyone still choose this direction when the signpost of fate indicates so many other more attractive locations, we always come back to three friends who seem to encapsulate the kernel of this whole conundrum.

Look at them and if you see anything of yourself within their tales, and you are

A Class Act

not already in the profession, then be afraid, be very afraid........

Nelson Rosario had a dream. In the dream, he was running in a meadow of lilies. As he trod the moist grass underfoot he heard the delighted screams of some children. Turning around, he spotted a group of ten year-olds in green uniforms, following him and pointing in his direction.

"Why are you following me?" asked Nelson, with surprise and a hint of joy. "Because you are our teacher" replied the children, "And you promised us a pound each if we did so."

On waking up from this sun-drenched epiphany, Nelson immediately contacted the relevant authorities and stood by his letterbox awaiting the application form for a teacher-training course.

Dean Charles had a stupendously high-earning job in London's financial centre, the square mile. He bought and sold futures. He didn't actually understand what this meant, but he knew that if he did it well, he got hefty bonuses. His colleagues were not only unfriendly, but peppered every snippet of dialogue, with competitive sneering. Seeking solace, he started talking to his computer terminal, but soon became frustrated by the pseudo-American twang of its replies.

One night after an impossibly fraught day spent hunched over his trading terminal, he made some life-changing decisions. For too long he had been singing the third above harmony with the spiritual god of money. He had lost the ability to open a packet of crisps and share them around. *Dammit,* he could afford every suit in the most exclusive of boutiques, but he couldn't even muster any small talk with the shop assistant. The following morning he consulted a careers agency, and one booklet leapt forth from the wooden shelving units: ***Starting a career in teaching***. He ran from the room possessed with a new zest for life and was promptly run over by a school bus.

Yolanda Monteith was lying in bed. The sun had risen hours before and was now beginning its slow descent behind the office blocks of Coventry. She was cradling the framed degree certificate which had been presented to her only three months previously, by a captain of industry whose name she had forgotten. She loved the look of the certificate, with its little waxy crest, and the mis-spelled name, *Yulandar Munteeth*. It had been signed by not one, but two eminent professors, and she clung to it now, more tightly than ever, desperate in her attempt to make it mean something in the eyes of the world. Three months a graduate and no job. And no

A Class Act

prospect of a job. When asked what it was she wanted to do by the incessant inquisitors in her mind, she could only shrug.

The dull ring of the phone, welled up from inside her duvet, and brushing her dried cereal bowl aside, she reluctantly lifted the receiver. It was her mum. "Darling, I've had an idea." Yolanda grimaced at this well-meaning opening. However, as her mum unveiled a plan, Yolanda's earlobes quivered gently, as she listened to what could amount to a whole life makeover. Yes, it was becoming so clear to her now. She was young, educated, unemployed...she should become a teacher!

Within seconds, she was sitting bolt upright in bed, and had arranged a preliminary visit to her local primary school, made easier by the fact that her mum was the Headteacher...........

Nelson, Dean and Yolanda all made their choices for very different reasons. Their tales help us to categorise the various routes into a teaching career, and we have drawn up three broad groups.

There are those like Nelson who follow the calling - a vision which may visit them in sleeping or waking hours, but a vision nonetheless, whose pull is so strong that to ignore it would be like omitting to buy a lottery ticket when an elf at the bottom of your garden has just told you the winning numbers for that night's draw.

Dean was clearly dissatisfied with work, and although he never got to teach his own class, there are many like him who arrive at teacher-training centres having pursued whole other lives as carpenters, opera singers or personal assistants to overfed middle-aged executives.

In Yolanda's case her graduate status was the launching pad to becoming a teacher, and although she suffered from a few months of uncertainty and melancholia, her newly won degree did open certain doors. That and her mother's good office of course.

If these are our chosen groupings, then let us look a little deeper at their make-up, because although our three friends have provided an insight into motivation for entering this particular profession, there are still questions to be asked, and tasks to be completed.

****

A Class Act

The Calling

Some people are going about their business just limescaling the bath with a new cleaning product, or thumbing through their junk mail library, when they are visited by what can only be described as a vision of saintliness. This vision is often so profound in its implications, that it amounts to a quasi-religious experience, and demands of the recipient total devotion and immediate action. It may take the form of a dream, as in the case of Nelson Rosario, but it has been known to leap forth from the pages of a totally unconnected text. For example, a car manual. Whichever way the message reaches you, it is loud and unequivocal, and it shouts in your tingling ear: *"You were born to be a pedagogue! Go forth and conjugate the verb to teach."*

The remarkable thing about the calling is the length of time it takes some people to respond. One elderly gentleman in Swindon was on his deathbed when he demanded to stunned relatives and a bewildered priest, that his last wish on earth was to feel the brush of chalk against a blackboard. Others don't wait *so* long, but do find themselves hankering after netball club well into their middle years.

The most earnest of individuals do respond at once, and there is the well documented case of Heather Benjamin, who left her house one breezy Thursday morning as an oceanographer, only to return seven hours later as a fully qualified early years teacher. Her voyage of discovery occurred as she took a short cut through the Safeway's car park. The stern looking attendant who stuck his head unreasonably far into her vehicle, ended his reprimand with the phrase, "Ever thought of being a teacher love?" It was a totally unplanned segment to his usual patter, and when subsequently questioned about the incident, the official's mind was completely blank.

For Heather though, it was an inspirational moment, and she sped to the local teaching college and ate several large theoretical volumes, thereby digesting in one foul swoop an entire year's worth of academic study. So impressed were the course tutors with this new study method that they not only provided her with a hastily prepared certificate but also stamped her forehead with her Department of Education number. Feeling elated and somewhat bloated, she staggered back to her house, delighted and ready to face her new life.

Heather's tale is slightly unusual, but the testimonies of countless others prove that the calling weaves its magic in a number of differing and sometimes bizarre ways. Whatever route the message does take, it is probably unwise to completely ignore it. If you are being called, but attempt to feign deafness, the consequences

A Class Act

can be severe. You can end up coaching a Sunday football team that involves making lengthy journeys on a hiding to nothing. Or you may find yourself squeezing in voluntary hours of weekend literacy support at your local library, when you could be making big-band compilation tapes.

If you are a parent and ignore the calling, you will most probably suffer from a compulsion to make your offspring sit behind desks reciting their number bonds whilst trying to watch *Grange Hill*. If you're not a parent, and decline to respond to the calling, you might find yourself suggesting to your partner that you start a family of thirty and invest in a king-sized whiteboard from the *Early Learning Centre*.

****

Dissatisfied with work

If you ever arrive at work with a feeling of intense dread. If the slightest quip from a colleague pushes you over the edge into the land of axe-wielding maniacs. If you wake up in a cold sweat each night screaming **"I AM NOT A BOX!"**...then you are clearly not satisfied with your work, and a change might be crucial. You may have been in a job for five years or five months. You may have entered this particular workplace with visions of lavish corporate entertainment and free holidays in the Seychelles. You may have had very few expectations, other than a quiet life and a regular pay cheque. However much you believed this job might work out, you realise that you have chosen incorrectly. Dean Charles was one such person, and had been trading in the city for seven years before he made his realisation. Douglas Swinton, got there a little quicker.

Douglas is a trainee retail manager. He's been on fruit and veg for three months now, and he knows his Royal Galas from his English Russets. He has a badge with his name on. There's a photograph of him behind the checkouts, resplendent in his blue uniform with orange piping. 'Happy to help' it says underneath his grinning head. But Douglas is far from happy. In fact, only last Monday Douglas came close to knifing a cantaloupe melon in a fit of pique. Even though he he knows that after his next stint on dairy, he will move to the back rooms of power (away from the shop floor where the air is purer, unfettered by the stink of cheesy milk) he is uneasy with the progress he has made in his short time with the company. His superiors assure him he is doing well. But Douglas feels his life is bereft of meaning. There are only so many Hass avocados you can price up in one lifetime.

A Class Act

Douglas feels he's already filled his quota. It is time for a change.

Douglas goes over in his mind a thousand ways of breaking the news to his grocery mentor, Steven. Should it be written in stringy celery stands or would a guava sculpture suffice? He knows he must leave, and yet he is anxious for an alternative as far away from the retail sector as is possible. It is while pondering these imponderables that he notices a young boy sticking his index finger deeply into a ripening aubergine. Without thinking, Douglas marches over to the reprobate, and gives him 100 lines and a week's detention in the tobacco kiosk. The penny drops. He must leave this shrine to shopping trolleys, and become a teacher - a good, old-fashioned disciplinarian.

He strides at once to the supervisors' lounge remembering to put down the tray of starfruits he is balancing on his head, and says on opening the door marked **NO ENTRY**: "I will send you this uniform, washed and ironed by return of post, but my resignation you can have now."

The experience of Douglas mirrors that of many in a vast range of jobs and professions. Doctors have been known to make the swift change from surgical mask to mortarboard. Gardeners have downed tools, and gone searching for science textbooks. Lawyers have removed wigs and begun spelling tests to the amazement of whole courtrooms.

What all of these people have in common is a desire to break entirely free from the shackles of their present employment, which they have come to believe is enslaving them in some way. They have arrived at the conclusion that going back to school on 'the other side' will offer them a more fulfilling and possibly liberating career choice. They may be right. They may be totally and hopelessly mistaken. Whatever the outcome, they are going to give it a go, and say a curt farewell to their old place of work.

A move into teaching certainly does represent a leap into the world of improvisation. It is a career that offers all of the thrills of stand-up comedy, without the fear of tanked-up hecklers bombarding you with advice in the form of flying beer glasses.

****

Graduates

A graduate is something more than an undergraduate. Something more than a graduand. But still a diploma short of a postgraduate. In short, it describes someone

A Class Act

who has managed by talent or trickery to convince some collegiate body somewhere to part with another certificate. This certificate is not the gateway to careers it used to be, but it can be an important prerequisite for securing a post. To enter the teaching profession you generally do need a degree, although in a changing world, there are access courses, shorter programmes of study and a host of new initiatives to bring different sections of the community into teaching, and these routes do pull in some of the finest teachers.

In the main though, recruits to teaching have either done a teaching degree (B.Ed), completed another degree, followed by the Postgraduate Certificate Of Education (PGCE), *or* have received a degree a while back, but have been mucking about for several years.

So what exactly is a graduate, and why are they more qualified to become a teacher than anyone else? To answer the second question first, they're not. To answer the first question requires a little more exploration.

A graduate by popular consent, is someone who has frittered away between two and four years (and possibly many more) sipping tea and talking absolute gibberish in a coffee bar which is called, eponymously, *The Coffee Bar*. On the long path to achieving graduate status, is essentially a lifestyle of uninhibited pleasure. A nine a.m lecture is viewed as anathema to one's entire existence, as is the doing of any work whatsoever. Free time is precious, and must be maintained at all costs. Thus, as graduation approaches, and the sanctioned freedom of student life trickles towards nothingness, thoughts turn towards the 'bad world out there' and more specifically to what jobs offer you the most tea breaks whilst providing you with a decent wage.

This frightening dilemma propels some towards the beckoning doors of the student career centre. The careers advisors are all ex-students who couldn't get any other jobs, and they smile at you in a welcoming, but slightly institutionalised fashion. There are booklets and folders for one to peruse, and you can spend many hours leafing through these and looking at the nice colourful pictures. It should be noted that careers literature works on the psyche in much the same way as that of estate agents' blurbs. Close your eyes and you are magically transported into the profession of your choice, working away happily, with no overdraft and a Sunday afternoon advert smile on your face. Inevitably, what the documents don't tell you, is that as an English graduate you have little chance of becoming a doctor. Still, we must all have our dreams.

You plough a lonely furrow, sitting on a moth-eaten chair in the corner of the careers centre, endlessly poring over a mound of publications. After hours of

A Class Act

deliberating, something has become crystal clear to you. You must stay within the student fold, to give yourself the chance of snuggling back into this lifestyle for another year. You must preserve your free time habits. You must not go straight out into the world of work. The teaching course to your mind, fits the bill very nicely. Sure, you skim over the pages about teaching practice in schools, and essay schedules, because you have picked up on the critical facts. It will be another year of studenthood, and successful applicants for the course receive the beauty of a grant.

You approach the nearest careers counsellor, and inform them of your reasoned choice. They may attempt to warn you that a year of teacher-training is unlikely to be like the rest of your student days, but you brush aside this wise observation and dance happily outside. Another destination called *The Coffee Bar* will be visited, another year of freedom beckons, another wonderful time will be had at the expense of the state.

Safe in the knowledge that your career path has been mapped out with all the accuracy of an AA Routefinder printout, you now cast haughty glances at your fellow undergraduates, sneering silently at their indecision. You have a destination to aim for, and they haven't yet reached the forecourt of the station. Having successfully applied to a teacher-training course through the central clearing system, the GTTR, you are able to live out the remainder of your undergraduate days in a haze of self-satisfied delirium. Whilst others wake to the hangover of a directionless world, you leap out of bed each day as you recall that your vocational travels are about to begin.

****

So there we are. We have outlined the three main groups that provide us with recruits to the profession. Sure, there are those who conform to none of them. There are a few people who have known since childhood that teaching is for them, either through the disciplining of younger siblings, or by taking an active interest in different handwriting styles. There are those who fell into the profession by chance or accident, and there are some who can't actually remember their reason for joining.

But, in spite of the terrible press the profession often receives, many others are still coming forward and saying, *I want a part of this*. Once on board though, what actually happens to those candidates on teacher-training courses? What are their fellow trainees like? And most importantly, can one get by without doing anything?

A Class Act

2. *What they should learn and how they should learn it*

The vacuum-packed year that is teacher-training

Salient fact about teacher training in the UK. You are guaranteed to get a grant. The grant is mandatory. Like the electric chair for murder in certain American states, it is metered out as a matter of policy and is enshrined in the tenets and principles of lofty nobility which date back to the inception of all things right and just. In the US the word 'mandatory' is forever linked in the minds of decent God-fearing citizens with the concept of swift justice. In the UK all rational, moral souls equate the word with a thrice-yearly cheque tardily delivered to the Bursar's office (up the stairs, second on the left). Somewhere in the world is a lost stone tablet decreeing all this, just waiting to be discovered. For many members of our species the deeply ancient mandatory status of the grant is a major contributory factor in choosing to train to be a teacher. In this vicious world, filled, as it is, with uncertainty and doubt, you know you can depend upon your local education authority to give an award.

And we like that. We think that's good.

How much longer funds will be made available for trainee teachers is anyone's guess, and by the time your eyes take in these words the notion of a grant may seem quaint, atrophied and not a little anachronistic. Just as the grants feed the students, so tuition fees feed the teacher-training institutions. In fact, teacher-training institutions could be viewed as benign parasites, living off this unique example of government magnanimity. Their sometimes trendy, progressive, 1960s, let's-sit-in-a-circle way of doing things may come in for a lot of flack.

The *Daily Mail* might want to publicly hang, draw and quarter every teacher-trainer. Yet, the mandatory nature of the grant has not yet been questioned by the establishment for fear of plague, pestilence and other Acts-Of-God. Hear ye, then, all would-be trainee teachers, hear these words of comfort and ebullient joy. If you get a place on a course, for the time being at least, the cheque's in the post. And that's a rare example of something being just as it should be. Democracy in action. A nation investing in its future.

Every year, then, since Jacob begat John-Julius, a splendid cohort of the UK's finest minds begin their initiation into the deeply complex modular form that is the teaching profession; These committed souls put aside their chances of earning big bucks in 'the City' in order to service the minds of future captains of industry, the

A Class Act

little Richard Bransons and Anita Roddicks dotted up and down this remarkable island who are getting to grips with the basic principles of laissez-faire economics, as tested at Key Stage 2.

So you 'go up' and what awaits you in the halls and seminar rooms? What mixture of social and educational ingredients are blended to guarantee the production of good quality teachers? To begin with you are given liberal doses of English and Mathematics. Teacher-trainers the length and breadth of the land know better than anyone the following fact:

During the 1970's and much of the 1980's no child was ever taught anything.

For this reason English, Mathematics and Science (but especially Mathematics) are fed to trainees intravenously throughout the course. An immediate assumption, often borne out by the looks of fear and loathing that pass across the faces of trainees when they hear the word MATHS, is that nobody, since about the time of Fermat (1601-1665), has been able to count or complete basic number operations.

For this reason all trainees are shackled to a core of subjects which mirror beautifully the structure of the national curriculum in schools. Lots of instruction on the important stuff - English, Mathematics and Science - with every other subject scattered round about like confetti, falling where chance decrees and having, perhaps, a brief moment devoted to their raison d'etre's.

The Trainee Teacher and Mathematics: a Case Study

What are eight sevens? Do you know? A recent report by the celebrated Skegness Institute of Applied Mathematics suggested that seven tenths of all graduate trainee teachers could not answer that question within the prescribed ten second time period. Moreover, of those seven tenths a further eight sixteenths, or to put it another way, half, were unable to answer the question 'what are nine sixes?'. It has been touted in certain circles that by the year 2020 a staggering 112% of the world's population of under twelves will be number illiterate.

This bodes ill for teachers and teacher-trainers, both of whom are already pencilled in by various organisations to take the blame.

Now, of course, all of these statistics and the doom laden projections of the *'Death of Maths'*, are quite simply utter nonsense. Everybody knows what eight sevens are,

A Class Act

just as everybody *doesn't* know the minute they're asked to answer the question on the spot. But the weight of the world's cares and woes lies heavily on the shoulders of our teacher-training institutions. There is an ever increasing expectation for things in schools to improve. Just as there is an almost constantly held belief among the latest generation of parents that 'standards', compared to their day, have irrevocably declined. Mathematics departments are quick to take note of such pressures and adapt accordingly. There are a whole host of examples:

In Lewisham this week, three members of faculty are carefully slicing the bodies of red mullet and making a display of the flesh, hoping to imbibe the principles of fractions in all those who file past the mass of fish heads and prime fillets. The slices, carefully marked off in twelfths, may well be entered for next year's Turner prize. More proof, if ever it were needed, of Mathematics' ability to be cross-curricular.

In the Cambridgeshire countryside, not too far from Huntingdon, fourteen lecturers from a local teacher training college are busily faking alien crop-circles in the belief that the constant appearance of the intricate designs in the local media will subliminally foster an appreciation of geometry among their intake of PGCE students. A bold plan, yet they have hopes for European funding next year.

Other, more traditional methods are employed in Southampton. The learning of tables by rote has taken a grip of the Maths tutors who can often be found pacing between the rows of desks set carefully in enormous squeaking gymnasiums, gripping the tops of gleaming golf clubs which rather than putting golf balls, chip circular fortune cookies onto the pupils' desks with a 'pop'. When unwrapped, the firm biscuits are found to contain powerful and accusatory messages. An example of one of these paper encouragements read: *"How dare you call yourself a mathematician! You're nothing but an inumerate flea with no algebraic qualities whatsoever in your pathetic soul. Perform an exercise in data-handling at once or be banished forever into the numberless wilderness."*

The list goes on. But rather than detail the advances in teacher training provision in the area of Maths in perpetuity, it is time we took a glance at this story from a different perspective. It is ripe for us to seek out the human angle. There follows a series of first-person accounts, transcribed from taped episodes of ethnographic observation which give a flavour of what the current intake of trainees make of the whole process of teacher-training. All participants have been anonymised so as not to affect future employment prospects.

A Class Act

Edited Transcripts

· "*I like the science lectures best. I was hopeless in science when I was at school. Couldn't get anything right. I was always the girl at the back whose experiment never got off the ground. No puffs of smoke or flashes of light. Nothing. Hopeless. My teacher didn't really explain where I'd gone wrong so I suppose I lost interest. But now I feel like I've got a second chance. Yesterday I demonstrated the Archimedes Principle in front of my group. I wrote it out as a lesson plan, did it all properly. On paper it looked perfect. But I was nervous about the practical part. In the end I needn't have worried. Everyone was really good about spending time in my bathroom. Teacher-training for me, well it's not just a training process. I'm learning stuff here I really should have grasped at school.*" **(Mabel, 26, Daventry)**

· "*The course is just about the biggest waste of taxpayer's money imaginable. We could have done all of the theory in an afternoon, and after two weeks teaching in a school we'd be ready. I'm fed up to the back teeth of arranging cereal packets on pieces of string to represent timelines.*" **(Debbie, 30, Southampton)**

· "*The tutors I like are the pragmatic ones. I don't want to know fifty different theories about how children learn. Quite frankly I couldn't care less about how the stuff goes into their brains. It's what they learn I'm interested in. What they learn, how quickly they learn it and does it stick? Simple as that - 1-2-3, no mucking about with all this Piaget nonsense. And as for Vygotsky, well, you know, when I'm in the classroom with thirty kids baying for blood that last thing on my mind if how to ensure they're all entering or about to enter the zone of proximal development.*" **(Roxy, 35, Preston)**

· "*Just before Christmas I thought I might drop out. It wasn't the essays or anything to do with the written work. I liked the days in college. I liked the other people on the course. It was the kids that were the problem for me. I didn't realise the job involved spending so much time with them. None of them say 'please' or 'thank you' and during my block of teaching practice one girl pulled a nasty face at me. If there's one thing I can't tolerate it's dreadful manners. I think I might go and do nannying at a finishing school in Switzerland instead.*" **(Bindia, 40, Chatham)**

· "*I was going to be a chef but it was just too fiddly. I didn't have the hands for it.*

A Class Act

Mind you I'm still fascinated in food preparation and want to share my love of the kitchen with any kids I teach. This training course is good. I drifted into it, but now I'm here I love it. The tutors are excellent, they really know their stuff and make it all interesting. Mind you, the canteen's not up to scratch and I insist on cooking my own lunch." **(Brian, 50, Dagenham)**

· *"Oh my God, teacher training! Don't tell me. I mean, it's such a dramatic year, full of triumphs and disasters. Exhausting too. You really long for the holidays. But the children make it. They're just so sweet. Darlings, absolute darlings. I've just finished my serial school visits for this term and I can honestly say it was one of the best experiences of my life. They made me a card and wrote a little song which Monica and Rachel sang to me. The parents even got me a bottle of Chablis and each one of them signed it. Everybody's just been tremendously helpful. Of course there have times when things have gone wrong. When Alastair took on a loose Doberman whilst I was on playground duty I really had quite a horrendous few night's sleep afterwards, I can tell you. He's fine though. And so will I be. I've had my termly 'down.' I think I'm due an 'up' sometime soon."* **(Ferdinand, 32, Keele)**

· *"You take your toilet roll tube and you make two little slits, like this, can you see? Then you take the foil you cut to size earlier and you wrap it round the tube, making sure you tuck the ends into the slits - like so. There. I'll show you the next part in a minute, I just need to find a strip of tissue paper."* **(Ahmed, 24, Bath)**

· *"The children are what make it. I suppose everyone says this, don't they? But, it's true. The children are what sticks out most in your mind. Certain individuals, usually the ones you would have dearly loved to strangle in the classroom. They're the characters, aren't they? You can laugh about it afterwards. It never seems quite as bad in hindsight. I remember the last time I saw Dane he was hanging from the classroom light flex, perfectly still, it was quite balletic really, holding a mallet above Rory's head, ready to drop it. I didn't see the funny side at the time. Dane was expelled. He's in a special school now. All the special kids get average schools and the Danes of this world, the way-below-average kids, they get the special schools. I asked a tutor about this. He told me to organise my school experience file."* **(Abbi, 28, Leeds)**

· *"It's just the best, man. I'm having a wicked time. I can't believe they're paying me to do this course. It's such a crack. I'd pay them to let me do this course, I really*

A Class Act

would. Except I'm skint. But it really is good. I haven't had to write a single essay yet and it's March already!" **(Dylan, 21, Newcastle)**

· *"What do I remember most? I remember on the first day some guy from the Skegness Council for Maths or something coming up to me and asking me what eight sevens were and I got it wrong. I said 54."* **(Tom, 22, East Sheen)**

The above glimpse of the student perspective illustrates well the ambiguity which surrounds the process of teacher-training in the minds of fledgling pedagogues. For some it is the catalyst they have been waiting for all their lives. An opportunity to effect change, to play a part in the shaping of our future society. For others it is a complete and utter waste of time, a farcical parody of truly good teaching.

Finding your first post

An important aspect of the teacher-training course is that, just as it reaches its climax, just as the workload is at its highest, just when you think the evening of coming home and falling asleep face down in a bowl of cornflakes will never end, you have an additional burden to bear. As well as teaching, being observed and writing everything up you have to set about the tricky business of finding your first job. This process is so much a part of the teacher-training course many collegiate handbooks now pencil in two weeks around March as a time when students are expected to speak in a hitherto unknown language and read the appointments section of the *TES*, twitching with anxiety lest they miss that mythical dream post in a school-with-no-children.

As a trainee teacher, the *TES* on Fridays, The *Guardian* on Tuesdays and The *Independent* on Thursdays become the holy trinity of texts. These papers hold the key to the meaning of life and you pore over them eagerly hoping that at any moment you will chance upon the dream job that no one else has spotted.

Of course, you soon realise the perfect school is a total fallacy. Like the precocious imp who questions religion because of the notion of the virgin birth, you begin to wonder whether these inky pages really have anything to offer you. Accordingly, you lower your sights.

You begin to entertain once more the notion of working in a school with children. You are tempted to go for one that is located in the depths of the countryside, though, where the pupils might still be twenty years behind their inner-city counterparts. Where they might still have some vestiges of respect for their

A Class Act

elders. Where they might still wear clothes and shun the supposed delights of inter-class feuding. There must be a job out there for you. Something. Somewhere. Every whisper you hear in every corridor seems to suggest that there is a golden nugget of an opportunity just waiting to be discovered. Your trawl through the sacred gospels of the *TES* one Friday lunchtime throws up this tempting insert:

CROWSWATER SPECIAL SCHOOL
Group 3S Day/Residential School
NOR 333 Age Range 3 -19

Required from September an enthusiastic and energetic teacher for a class of KS1 pupils. Opportunities for professional development will be regularly provided. The school is set in 350 acres of Welsh countryside and has its own gym and outdoor swimming pool.

This is it, you tell yourself. A new beginning in a far off land, miles from anywhere and sports facilities thrown in. A far cry from the urban misery of your teaching practice school, with its fortified windows and heavy duty locks on the computer room. Suddenly you feel born again and you rush to the phone to obtain application forms. You dial the number. Your hands are trembling. This is history in the making. The first day of the rest of your life. Someone picks up at the other end. You think you can hear someone's voice. But you're not sure.

"*Hello?*" you venture. "*Hello?*"
"*Bore da.*"
"*Hello, I'm phoning about the Key Stage 1 post.*"
"*Bore da.*"

You put the phone down and shred the *TES*.

Many trainee teachers begin to feel the urge to seek employment abroad during that final Easter of the course. The wonders of Prague, Bermuda, Sao Paulo, all beckon tantalisingly from the back pages of the appointments section. You could bear the surly children if it was sunny all the time, you tell yourself. Switching attention from Metropolitan Wigan you flirt with the idea of The British School in Japan or the United World College of South East Asia in Singapore. Finally you settle for St. Peter's School in Nassau, the Bahamas. The school even has an e-mail address. You

A Class Act

are convinced this is the place for you - you will be a shoeless teacher to the children of tax-evading rock superstars and their entourages, scribing pie charts into the slivery sands of the beach with a bit of driftwood.

Weeks pass by and then one fateful morning a fat envelope arrives asking you to attend an interview. Inside you find a map of the island, a list of hotels and some English phrases translated into Spanish. But no air tickets. You tip the envelope upside down and shake it vigorously. Still no air tickets. You make an appointment to see your bank manager. You show her the letter. You ask for another overdraft extension. She laughs at you. You go home and microwave the letter.

In fact after all the aborted attempts to flee the confines of your college and its partnership schools you are offered a post in your teaching practice class. You sigh at the inevitability of it all but secretly warm to the idea of being able, at long last, to pay off the mountain of debts that casts a shadow over your home, car, clothes and fridge magnets. You are not entirely sure what you have learnt about teaching over the duration of the course. But you completed it, and in your frazzled state of mind, that seems to be reason enough to smile. Your class of teaching practice pupils cheer when they are told of your appointment, not because they respect your educational prowess, but because it gives them a whole summer to prepare innovative forms of mayhem for one whom they know is new to the profession.

Can you train teachers?

So can you train teachers or not? Can you feasibly prepare a cohort of adult men and women for the infinitely variable nature of schools and the behaviour of pupils within them? Or are you reciting your creed like a mouse in the face of a force 10 gale? If training does offer something vital in the preparatory process is it best undertaken in colleges and schools or schools alone? Are teachers born or made? Nature or nurture? Instinct or instruction? Questions which lead to further questions. The doubtful worth and value of one thing means the questioning of the worth and value of another thing.

Maybe it's all about finding out what type of teacher you are, what type of person you are, just *who* you are. In this way, teacher-training is a languorous therapy session that just stretches on and on, and which you're paid to attend. What could be more edifying than that? A voyage of discovery, a course of travel around your own sensibilities, a jaunt to which you and you alone are appointed tour guide - with the beautiful reality that the state has paid for your return ticket.

A Class Act

3. *On remand for good behaviour*

The teacher's probationary year

Probation n. 1. a system of dealing with offenders by placing them under the supervision of a probation officer. 2. on probation. a. under the supervision of a probation officer. b. undergoing a test period. 3. A trial period as for a teacher - probational or probationary adj.

Can you imagine Aristotle's probationary year? Or Plato's? Two bearded sages quivering with fright as they chiselled out a tick on ancient registers of stone. Great teachers have always stared down the precipice of fear that is their first year in the profession. Socrates was as unsure of his ability to control a class as you or I. As long as culture has existed, teachers new to the job have fretted over their ability to swim in the fast flowing river of Lifelong Learning, a stream into which they were hitherto compelled to merely dip their toe. Down through the ages a lineage of probationary year uncertainty exists and can be traced back through examples of classroom practice, thus illustrating the commonality of experiences amongst all new teachers, in all eras.

Aristotle, to take one of the undisputed 'Greats' as our example, was petrified when given his first class, known then as the First Academy. The night before his first day teaching in a little stone-floored room off the Agora, he looked up into the night sky, his head pounding with anxiety. He could feel his feet sweating profusely, despite being clad in flip-flop sandals. The stars were bright in the heavens and he espied Orion's Belt. "Oh, Orion," he said meditatively, "Grant me the skill to control my class and to plan and prepare thoroughly each lesson. Let my long and medium term planning be kept up to date and let there be no wet breaks until after the mid-winter feast of Apollo."

On the first day of school Aristotle woke early and began a series of stretching exercises. He breakfasted on olives and bread. Then, armed with a brain awash with wisdom he began the short journey to the schoolroom. His trepidation turned to terror when he saw his class of boys for the first time. They had set up opposing battle lines at either end of the room and were using wooden swords and window shutters to re-enact the battle of Troy. When one particularly boisterous youth known as Alexander saw the new sage he exclaimed: "Ah, Mr Tabernacle! We've been expecting you. And I see from your size and deportment that you are perfect for the part of the Trojan horse. On your knees, please, sir." To his own

A Class Act

astonishment Aristotle found himself getting down onto his hands and knees, suppliant before the boy's prodigious force of character. Alexander was pleased by this subservience and took an instant liking to his new teacher.

Several years later, the mock battle just ended, Aristotle waved goodbye to his first class, happy that he had fulfilled an academic and pastoral role. He felt sure Alexander would do well and it came as no surprise when news of his former pupil reached him some years afterwards, describing how he had carved out a huge empire and was busily naming cities after himself. This proliferation of 'Alexandrias' and the way the young man had been dubbed 'Great,' Aristotle found both vulgar and charming.

In Aristotle's story we have the essence of the probationary year. Frolicking, a little marking, inspirational teaching, some planning, a bonding with certain special pupils and the poignancy of that first goodbye. Not much has changed since the days when all teachers, regardless of sex, wore long, flowing white robes and patriarchal beards.

In the modern world the probationary year entitles new teachers to certain privileges and rights - a free period now and again to plan and prepare lessons and some in-service training to back up the theory injected at college. However, various Conservative governments viewed such bonuses as a flagrant waste of tax-payers money and thus the tag 'probationary year' gave way to the term 'Newly Qualified Teacher' (NQT). Under this system the more unscrupulous employers were able to let go of a newly qualified teacher at the end of their first year, only to employ another fresh faced college leaver, thus making a saving on their wage bill. However, the more magnanimous local education authorities continued to offer NQT's the old style probationary year with time-out from the classroom built into their timetables.

So, what exactly is the probationary or NQT year? And does it truly test your aptitude for a career in teaching? In answer to this question one thing is clear. For the first time you really are on your own and there is no one sitting in the corner who may be consulted. It's your first cohort of children; your first class of thirty. Those names inked up so neatly on your class register will become etched so deeply into your memory that many years hence, when you are seated on a sofa in a rest home and a doctor asks who you are, you will in all probablility offer him a choice from this list of thirty.

Most NQT's do have fond memories of their first batch of chicklings. Most NQT's do have a good war. One experienced teacher from Hackney recently related her first emotions on walking into her inaugural class: *(Wistfully)* "I walked through

A Class Act

the gates on that first morning full of hope and spirit, glad to see the likely looking boys kicking a football about. I'll soon lick them into shape, I thought. No ball control and a woefully undeveloped sense of positional play. I turned the corner and walked up the three steps to the prefab that was to serve as my home for a year. It was locked. I went home and never returned."

Such reminiscences are out of the ordinary but that first year is a time of experimentation and radical educational innovation. Within one school in Shropshire an NQT shut out the strained world beyond her classroom door by informing her pupils that their class had become part of a space research project. In one particularly beautiful lesson they turned the reading corner into a space shuttle. They sat motionless in their chairs looking skyward (though the ceiling somewhat limited their view) for three days and nights counting down the moments until take-off. Then they started silent reading.

That first 'solo' year provides the opportunity to discover what sort of a teacher you are. Are you an authoritarian voice-raiser? Or a do-as-you-please child-friendly teacher? A chalk and talk proponent, or a scissors and glue practitioner? Will you insist on silence during certain lessons, or do you enjoy the insistent hum of children at work? Do you execute detention at break- time or do rush into the playground screaming *"I'm in goal you sad-assed muthas"*? However much you learn on your pathway through a teaching career the die is cast very early.

In those local Authorities offering some in-service training for NQT's, induction courses usually take place in education centres. These structures in which an interior designer has been allowed to run riot, house upright pianos, echoing corridors and a stealthy janitor. As any NQT will testify you soon establish a love-hate relationship with these learning honey pots. On the one hand you love them because every Thursday afternoon you know that come sea-swell or high winds you will be released from your classroom to attened another session. Your children will be left in the care of an inept supply teacher and thus will love you a little more on your return. On the other hand you hate the induction courses because you feel that you've already plumbed the depths of theoretical boredom within your time at a teacher- training institution.

The induction courses take place in a mock classroom setting with participants residing on faux-armchairs, their eyes glazing over and bic pens dropping from their feeble grasps. The two hour sessions are often delivered by a hippie at the front.

Ah, yes. The hippie at the front. Don't be fooled by the suit and municipal shoes. Your course leader is a classic post-modern hippie - a warm supportive, touchy-

A Class Act

feely type who for the sake of career advancement has donned the garb of the professional classes. The kaftans and beads may be gone, but the spirit of free love still hangs heavy in the air.

"**Teaching is loving, it's an unconditional act of giving...**"

"**Shall we unpick that last statement?**"

"**I want you to turn to the person next to you and...share.**"

"**Sight is only one of the five senses. We can also use our sense of smell to read.**"

"**Your scheme of work shows me pain.**"

Sentiments such as these drive many NQT's into a pattern of Thursday afternoon absenteeism that most education welfare officers would find alarming. Teachers go missing from induction courses because they are more interested in studying the decor of a local cafe or going home early to catch up on some much needed sleep.

The NQT year has given rise to several major news stories. One in particular is worthy of exploration, although it only managed to secure the brief '...and finally' slot on the ITN Network. At the time it was billed simply as a minor explosion on the sit of a Derbyshire Education Centre. The newsworthy angle lay in the fact that Derek, the site caretaker swore he had witnessed three ghostly apparitions just prior to the blast. Bearing in mind that the site had formerly housed a monastery it was considered worthy of inclusion for broadcast.

At the epicentre of the story were three NQTs from a small rural primary school who were attending a session on 'The Delivery of the Science Curriculum.' As teachers new to the profession they were keen to bring their own brand of knowledge to bear on the National Curriculum. One of their number was deeply interested in the medieval notion of witches and had talked the other two into holding meetings on the school playing fields after dark, where much babbling took place around a cast iron cooking pot. This particular individucal was also mildly dyslexic and when he received the course handbook misread this particular lecture title as 'The *Devilry* of the Science Curriculum.'

Thus, on the appointed day these three colleagues arrived at the education centre armed with piles of literature concerning witchcraft. They were appalled to find that their tutor maintained a steadfastly orthodox approach to science. Incensed by his

A Class Act

one-sided appraisal of what the science curriculum should include, the three stormed out of the session and began circling the building. Chanting incantations and pouring petrol on the walls they danced with swift movements. As the flames began to slide around the Victorian brickwork it provided the caretaker Derek with a golden opportunity to appraise the efficiency of his fire drill. He managed to douse the flames and evacuate the building in spite of his terror at seeing the three strange figures bearing down towards him.

The whole matter was hushed up by the local authority and to this day the identities of the 'Derbyshire Three' remain shrouded in mystery. There are strong indications however, that they now run a vacuum cleaner repair business near Settle, Yorkshire.

Other tales of probationary woe serve as honest reminders to those unsure about whether or not to become a teacher. Madeline Herriot was a myopic woman who was appointed to a post at an inner city school in Cardiff. On the first Wednesday of her probationary year a tragedy was luckily averted when the Deputy Headteacher happened to step into Madeline's classroom. Her pupils were watching in horror as Miss Herriot began an internal examination of the school cat, Molly. The Deputy Head pulled the probationer off her feline charge before the children's minds became polluted by the scene that may have followed. On questioning Madeline later that same day it became clear that she had understood she was now a practising vet and that the children, with their array of flourescent knapsacks, were a flock of particularly eloquent parrots. On realising her error she underwent corrective laser surgery and now lectures on animal husbandry in New Zealand.

NQT's are often told that one phrase above all should be their mantra. *Don't smile till Christmas* is a sentence that preys on many minds new to classroom practice. Probationers are informed that by looking serious for three months, pupils will hang onto their every word and not talk when they are talking. For some, sticking rigidly to this behavioural choice earns then the nickname 'stoneface" amongst both staff and pupils. For others, it causes strain within certain groups of facial muscles. It is clear that an NQT must lay down the law as soon as they take up their first job. It is no good trying to befriend the children or get onto their level in the hope that this will provide a calm classroom atmosphere. If the boundaries are not established immediately then the children will literally run riot.

Many NQT's choose to establish a system of rules on their first day. For some these have already been written and are non-negotiable. They include items such as: *Never leave your place without asking* and *don't look at the teacher unless you're given permission*. The more liberal NQT engages in a democratic process of jointly

A Class Act

establishing a legal framework. In this way the children are involved in shaping the class structures and rules. This can cause problems as some children think "I can only hit people when I'm cross" is an acceptable peramater of legislation. Each teacher is different and each will decide upon their own happy medium.

An NQT must also decide how they are going to conduct themselves amongst the staff group. Some attempt to immediately ingratiate themselves with colleagues by playing practical jokes on them and offering spring vacations to log cabins in the Swiss Alps. Others choose a more aloof approach and deliberately ignore everyone. The latter stance can cause severe communication diffculties as no one actually has the courage to approach a seemingly untouchable new memeber of staff. In one example of this phenomenon, in the run up to the Easter holidays, a Headteacher meekly asked an NQT what form of assessment she had been completing for the previous six months. "What's assessment?" replied the NQT. "You'd better sit down, dear," the Head explained, consolingly. "There's a bit of paperwork you need to catch up on."

The first year can be an extremly shocking experience. The mere caseload of paperwork can be very off-putting to the new teacher. There are portfolios of work to be amassed, reading records to be finished, observational notes to be taken and displays to be mounted. The sheer amount of tasks to be completed can lead the NQT to spend very late nights on the school premises, leaving the building only when the caretaker taps his watch at the window. The steady stream of other staff out of the building at reasonable times is impossible to understand. How can they do it all so quickly? When do they find time to fit everything in?

Many though, do enjoy the challenges and like nothing better than making their classroom a model of interactive excellence, but others find the experience humbling and a trifle lonely. One aspect of class life that can freak out even the most restrained of professionals is the necessity to hear every child read on a weekly basis.

If each child is heard and assessed for approximately ten minutes then this can constitute up to five hours of work. If this time is to take place within the classroom, then the teacher is going to need long periods of silence within the week. This is very hard to achieve in many classrooms, and common is the sight of the NQT yelling at their class for quiet as they are trying to listen to a pupil read. Some teachers create sound proof boxes that they climb into with a reading group and can thus ensure a modicum of silence. The downside to this set up is that the other children can effectively do whatever they please when the teacher is concealed

A Class Act

within the box.

Within the craziness of this first year it can be very easy for the new teacher to forget what the term 'social life' means. Colleagues will continually tell them to 'get out of the house a bit more' or, more worryingly 'get a life.' The problem for the NQT is that they do have a life that has been ordered and prepared for them. If they are to keep up with even the most basic rudiments of classroom management, hours of time need to be put in. The skills of time-management and corner cutting are unfortunately only learnt through experience and thus it is still a few years before they can put their feet up.

The probationary year can be a very affirmative experience because new teachers are not sated with the cynicism of many of their more experienced colleagues. Bold, innovative teaching techniques can be introduced. Children can be inspired by the fiery passion of an energetic probationer.

Take, for instance, Janet Huckleberry. She had a quite remarkable probationary year. In her Lancashire primary school she began a series of inspirational engineering lessons which culminated in her class building a bridge spanning the gap between the school playing fields and the local fish and chip shop.

This not only covered many of the Maths attainment targets whilst simultaneously fostering group work and a sense of citizenship. It also regenerated trade at *The Jolly Codman Fish Bar* which in turn had a knock on effect, increasing sales in the nearby newsagent and antiques shop. Huckleberry was interviewed by a local television news programme and remarked:

"This is my first year of teaching and I suppose I wanted to make my mark, really. You know, show the parents and pupils that I am a capable professional. My tutor at college has been a great source of inspiration. Oh, he's wonderful feller, Mr Kingdom-Brunel, and he's got smashing handwriting."

These are testing times for education, not least because the best ways to test teachers and their general aptitude for the profession is one fraught with disagreement. For the time being the first year as a full time class teacher, whether it's termed a probationary year or not, remains a time of mutual appraisal. A period in which the worryingly incompetent can be gently eased out of schools and into other, less sensitive areas of social life. Simultaneously it allows the truly talented to shine, and to push at the boundaries of what constitutes current acceptable educational practice.

If you survive a year with your appetite for schools and life still intact, then you

A Class Act

were probably made to be a teacher and can begin pedalling on a cycle of elation and despair which, in its emotional complexity, only seasoned pedagogues can appreciate.

A Class Act

4. Interview with Tim Brighouse

Professor Tim Brighouse taught history in Grammar and Secondary Modern Schools. He entered education administration in what was then Monmouthshire in 1967. He served for two years as Deputy Chief Education Officer for the now defunct Inner London Education Authority, and for ten years held the post of Chief Education Officer for Oxfordshire. Concerned about what he perceived as the turbulent times ahead for teachers and administrators, he took up a post lecturing in Education at Keele University. In September 1993 he decided to return to the fold and took up a post as Chief Education Officer for Birmingham LEA, where he remains today. In March 1999 he resigned as Co-Vice-Chair of the government's Standards Task Force. He has written in a wide variety of newspapers and journals, and has been an outspoken critic of the current Ofsted regime.

When Tim Brighouse's secretary rang to confirm he would grant an interview, we could hardly believe our luck. He is one of the most in-demand figures on the British educational scene, undertaking countless administrative, writing and speaking committments each year. He is widely regarded in teaching circles as a sensible, constructive supporter of those in the teaching profession.

JZ: How can disadvantaged schools be really helped? Is there some need for a radical overhaul of the way the per pupil funding works, should extra teachers be given to schools in terrible circumstances, are we needing a radical solution on this one?

TB: I think there is room within the formula providing you weight poverty sufficiently, sensitively and well. That's to say, there is a world of difference between a school say with sixty per cent of free school meals and thirty per cent free school meals and it's more than double, if you see what I mean, so you need to have a geometric weighting. But you can within the formula find a way of rewarding that. Diffferent authorities do it in different ways.

We don't weight it sufficiently highly because we've inherited a system which didn't allow us to do that at the time, we've been desperately trying to improve it since. I do think that you need more resources, whether it's teachers and learning assistants, and I would personally go for every teacher having a learning assistant.

A Class Act

I'd be wanting to weight that in areas of socio-economic disadvantage.

JZ: Could there be an argument in some schools to actually have two teachers in a class where there's huge behavioural problems, maybe with one helping in the management of behaviour and one doing the teaching. Or would that just not be financially viable anywhere?

TB: First of all teachers working together is fine - more than one in a room that seems to be excellent, I've seen good team teaching happen, I wouldn't do it for the discipline thing I think you're barking up the wrong tree, moreover I think a learning assistant alongside a teacher is an excellent idea, a well trained learning assistant.

JZ: What do you think of the implementation of the national literacy strategy and do you think this prescriptive way of imposing things on teachers is the way forward?

TB: It seems to me that everyone getting behind a literacy strategy together is a good idea. I'm going round saying you've got not to regard this as a straitjacket, there's some wonderful materials, tinker with it, move it change it, own it, learn from each other and try and sing roughly the same tune because that's a powerful ingredient which shifts a school. I think the way it has been implemented shows lack of knowledge of the management of change and I don't put that down to ministers, I put that down to officials who really don't understand it.

We got last week our targets for reducing exclusions and improving attendance. Last paragraph of the letter said authorised attendance, and it said something like: we realise that unauthorised attendance could go down simply by Heads authorising absence, but we'll be on the lookout for that and we've told Ofsted to report on it, so we'll hold you accountable.

So I wrote back and said: 'really really good to get your letter and it's one of those I didn't reply to for a day because I might get really angry, but you could reword that couldn't you by saying, we know Heads cheat, we're going to make Ofsted observe, and we'll hold you responsible for them cheating. Is that the message you wish to convey?' I don't put that down to ministers, because ministers do not read a letter like that, but it is a total misunderstanding of how you motivate people.

A Class Act

JZ: My concern about advanced skills teachers is that only a few could be given the grading. It couldn't be an across the board thing?

TB: Well we need a different pay structure. I'd be wanting to pick out the absolute stars, but I'd certainly be wanting to reward those in the profession who stay a time and are seen to be highly competent. At the moment the pay of teachers suffers because there are 450,000 of them. If there were not 450,000, if there were 45,000 they would be paid amazingly.

JZ: Teachers are sometimes pointed at for being whingers and moaners and when Mr. Woodhead got a substantial pay increase and the review body was recommending 2.5 per cent for teachers. There was a whole brouha. Is that sort of thing a complete red herring, or should teachers be voicing their concerns?

TB: I'm not really very much in favour of performance related pay, so I'm not in favour of this business of people being paid bonuses for their performance in a particular year. The only bonus I would have, is if you could prove that the lot of those performing least well in the system has substantially improved and you could demonstrate there was a direct connection between what you'd done and what they'd achieved, then I think they should get a pay rise. But I don't think that's very likely. I'm not in favour of pay rises for very well paid people and I include myself in that.

JZ: Would you accept that under the previous Conservative administrations there was some sort of agenda of teacher-bashing, whatever you want to call it. There was an agenda whereby teachers were seen as being politicised and they had to be challenged. There was about 15 or 16 years of teachers being put down. Is that a fair analysis of the Conservative years, or were there people in there who were genuinely committed to education?

TB: I'm sure people wanted education to succeed, but they believed they could make it succeed by accentuating the negatives, and I think that this government came in and inherited that, and at least for a while, those around them have continued to behave in the same way.

I personally believe you get the best out of people by building on relationships, introducing targets from the bottom up, not top down, resourcing things, backing things, working on good things and dealing with problems in a proper balance and dealing with failure in private.

JZ: In terms of the Labour government, do you think they're doing enough, or are going to do enough to assure teachers that they're truly working in partnership with them?

TB: I think the government is really genuinely interested, David Blunkett and Estelle Morris in particular, are genuinely interested in getting behind the teachers, encouraging them, building on the energy, trying really hard. I think they're trapped within a system, where after 15, 18 years of DfEE civil servants and other agencies where that hasn't been the prevailing culture.

I think it's tremendously difficult to turn a big organisation like that round. I think they're trying to do it, I think they're making noble efforts, they've got more resources into the system, they're trying to examine the issues that need examining, but they've got quite a long way to go yet.

JZ:Taking something like the league tables. How damaging do you think the non value-added league tables have been?

TB: It depends where you are in the country. In some parts of the country people haven't got much choice of school anyway and it hasn't mattered a bit. In areas where there is a great pecking order, then it's accentuated the position in the pecking order, and its made those at the bottom having to work even harder to catch up than they would have done before.

JZ: And what about moves to introduce value-added league tables. Do you think that will make a big difference?

TB: You need statistics, you need information in order to benchmark where you are with others and improve, and the issue is not so much are the league tables the right thing? I'm all for the value-added stuff, but the big issue is how rapidly you're improving. In Birmingham, I'm glad there's a great emphasis on how well we're doing with regards to every other LEA.

I get worried about this every year. I visit other LEA's, I learn from their experience.

A Class Act

I'm trying every bit to try to make sure our schools improve faster than in every other place. So I've got a vested interest.

I don't mind Birmingham being in a league table. I don't think that's affecting individual kids. It will affect whether we attract good teachers, and frankly I think we've got a good enough reputation that people would want to come to us. It doesn't do us any harm at authority level. It doesn't do us any harm at a national level. At a school level, it begins to be harmful.

School level information in published form, if treated crudely, is not useful. In published form, so that schools can learn off each other and improve on good practice, it's very useful.

JZ: Sometimes the information is used crudely in local papers. In Birmingham if there is a problem of morale, what sort of strategies for improving morale do you use for teachers and schools?

TB: You'd be better asking them wouldn't you, because it's all going to sound alright when I tell you. You sit up late, you write handwritten notes to teachers, if I've written one letter to an indivual in the five years I've been here, I've written three or four thousand. Advisers are asked to tell me about not good practice, but generosity of spirit - people walking the extra mile, doing really good things. If they tell me about it, I'll write a handwritten note. I think that's the least I can do because teachers are working really really hard. You would try, and if a school's in trouble, I would go to a school and visit the staffroom. You do loads of inset.

JZ: It seems at times in the educational world that you've stood up alone. Do you feel that you personally have a role to stand up on political and educational issues?

TB: I think that I'm always afraid that I'll be the dog that didn't bark in the night. Now that's dangerous because you might bark too often. I'm always worried if you didn't say what you thought. I really am certain that David Blunkett and Estelle Morris are people of goodwill, but they're in a machine which they've somehow or other got to make sure doesn't undermine them.

JZ: Is that possible?

A Class Act

TB: Any organisation can shift. The DfEE has changed. Things are capable of being shifted. What you surely have to do is attempt all the time to shift it. Birmingham, as an education authority, isn't nearly as good as it should be, so you're bending every sinew trying to shift it in directions that will unlock a bit of energy here or a bit more energy there.

I'm about to write to a number of Heads about how you make every school feel unique. How do you do that? Within a classroom it's that that makes a difference to a kid. And the best schools make every member of staff feel that about themselves.

JZ: I'd like to ask some questions about the raising of standards in reference to the current Ofsted regime. It seems to me, that when a school is working in a climate of social, economic and cultural adversity, they're being criticised in Ofsted reports, or actually failed if they're not achieving SATs results in line with local or national averages. I know in Birmingham, that's been the case with some of your own schools. Does an Ofsted report provide a fair analysis of a school's success?

TB: It can do but it often doesn't. You have to ask whether the system and whether Ofsted inspections are reliable and bring a test to them of the validity of what they're up to. There are lots of other questions you might ask, whether they're value for money and whether they discharge accountability, and around the line you're interested in, is whether they're developmental or not.

Around the reliability bit, there is stronger evidence that they aren't reliable, and I think that's down to the fact that their training programmes are cursory, and that their vetting of new applicants to be Ofsted inspectors leaves quite a bit to be desired. We know of people about whom had we been asked to write a reference, we couldn't have recommended.

Or we know of people who have left schools in not very good circumstances and who then subsequently have become inspectors. It seems to me, that because they expanded things so rapidly, they drew into the system variable quality. When they are let loose on schools as it were, because of that variable quality and because there's no sufficient substantial effort made to moderate their judgements, then it seems to me, there's a kind of whimsicalness in the judgements made by various Ofsted teams.

A Class Act

JZ: In other words there's an irony here. They have a very strict set of criteria for judging schools, yet they are not sticking rigidly to the same standards.

TB: I don't think they have sufficiently rigorous standards to monitor the quality of their own teams. I think they've got extremely good at monitoring the quality of the reports that are written, but that isn't necessarily a sufficient rigour in the quality of the processes that are involved, nor of the judgements that are being made. And we're all in a difficult position on this, because uniquely in my experience they're not prepared to share the evidential base on which they make the judgements.

JZ: What about the situations like, there was a school recently in Birmingham which didn't achieve SATs results in line with national averages, but is really fighting economic and social problems, and yet they're still getting criticised in the report, whereas someone like yourself could say they should be lauded, they're getting fifty per cent of kids achieving the right level in English, that's amazing.

TB: You read in lots of primary school reports that the standards achieved in foundation subjects are below national expectations. Well the fact is, nobody knows any national standards and nor are the inspectors trained in terms of the foundation subjects. About the only things you could say that about would be those which are subject to SATs tests. That in itself is a flaw. I don't want to be driven into a corner to saying that a school that achieves fifty percent at level 4 is doing well, it depends on the circumstances. It may well be that they're not doing well. Things like mobility may be an issue, which as far as I can see is not taken into account in their judgements, and which should be.

What I'm always looking for is that a school is improving and that it can demonstrate it's improving both within the proccesses it applies and the outcomes that are achieved by the kids. I don't want to get painted into a corner of saying even in the most adverse of circumstances you can't achieve: You can and some schools are demonstrating this. It's the reverse that worries me.

I have yet to see any schools that are regarded as being in need of special measures in very favourable areas. Some teachers get an excellent report while teaching in one area, but a poor report when they're teaching in another area.

JZ: Do you think that Ofsted has done quite a lot of damage to teacher morale? In some cases schools do take quite a long time to return to normal after an Ofsted inspection week. Is there a way the system could be improved?

TB: I think the system could be substantially improved. I've criticised it in terms of reliability, I just don't think there's a consistent standard between the teams, nor even within one team in differing circumstances on differing days. I do believe that the system is damaging, particularly to schools that require lots of energy to make them successful, and they are, by definition in my view, urban schools, where I think the energy required by the staff is phenomenal, it needs to be relentless. I mean achieving a sense of pace which everybody agrees is really important, seems to be far more difficult in hostile circumstances than it does in circumstances where the community pressure and the peer group pressure is towards achievement.

I'm absolutely sure that we are witnessing two things. One is teachers in heavily urbanised areas, burning out. And I think the Ofsted process is going to accelerate that, and I can point to cases of particular teachers who, following a reasonable Ofsted report which said that their efforts are satisfactory, have, because they've been putting hours in which means that they've got nothing to do with their lives other than work, have said 'OK well if that's all I can be, I'm going to do something else.' I can quote chapter and verse teachers who have done that. That's really serious.

The second thing is, I could take you to teachers who have been identified as outstanding, but are working in a school labelled as special measures, and after three years of trying to get the school out of special measures, the school has not succeeded, but on every visit have been consistently told that they themselves are outstanding, have now gone onto other schools and are now actively seeeking to leave the profession.

JZ: When Ofsted have given numbers of failing teachers, are these numbers suggested to frighten the profession, or are there really say thirteen to fifteen thousand failing teachers?

TB: You can ask the question because by now there must be so many reports that will have identified how many failing teachers there are that it should now be beyond question. They have got all those figures, so the question should be asked. As far as the figures are concerned, I don't personally believe that the figure's

A Class Act

thirteen to fifteen thousand.

JZ: Many teachers feel under attack from Ofsted and government with the media used to expound such views. Do you think it is the case that they have been under attack, and if they have been under attack, should they be answering back in some way?

TB. I think it's ever so complex, because I think that our society is expecting more and more from schools and teachers. We're living in an age of information technology, creativity, education is tremendously important. We're moving upmarket in the need for education training and skill. That's the context. The school is the only institution they can invest in to do something about that. Kids are only in school for fifteen per cent of their waking time. More and more is heaped on the school and expected of the school.

I think this government, quite helpfully is talking about education beyond the school. The media has become very very strong, and in a democracy, it's almost become too strong in terms of influencing public opinion, rather than reflecting public opinion. If you were a politician you would have to be mindful of that and teachers themselves are a small part of the electorate.

Parents on the other hand are quite a large part of the electorate and probably need reassurance that their school's OK but isn't it great that their kids aren't in a school that isn't OK. And I think that that doesn't help, and I think we've lived through a period which I hope is coming to an end, where there seems to be a belief that you can improve things through fear. I don't believe that. I believe that you improve things by what I would call appreciative inquiry.

If you look at the summary at the end of all those Ofsted reports - points for action, every one of them are problems that they've got to address. You and I have got problems every day when we get up, at the end of the day we run out of energy because we think 'I can't go on', whereas I think what's required is creation of energy and you create energy by identifying what's good as well as dealing with the problems.

You can't forget the problems but what I think you need is a balance here. I think the machine of government - the DfEE, Ofsted - it's a regulatory state, it's not well

A Class Act

suited to firing the imagination, the energy of teachers.

JZ: In the classroom if you're always negative to children you get a poor response.

TB: You do.

JZ: If your despair is with Ofsted what can be done about Ofsted. Is there anything that teachers could be doing?

TB: I think we all have to dispassionately point out ways in which Ofsted can be reformed and improved. As it happens I'm just producing a paper which I will give to the House of Commons Select Committee. I will try to make sure that an alternative and better system is continually brought into the arena to be discussed. There are ways in which you can improve the system. There are ways you could easily spend less money, and have a more developmental and more reliable system that would still leave the schools totally accountable and you would be unlocking energy instead of wasting it.

JZ: Is there a problem with Chris Woodhead himself, or is it the whole mechanism of Ofsted has to shift ?

TB: It looks to me as though Chris is much more prepared to change his mind than Duncan Graham ever would have been. It may well be that he's perfectly prepared to shift the climate and I certainly don't think it's the person, I don't want to get into the person, I just think the system needs to be shifted to being more developmental and less punitive, and more reliable. It would be so easy to do. All you really need to do is go to every primary school in this country and say 'right an Ofsted inspection is coming up, have a look at the last report. What is the report that you'd like written on yourself?' This would encourage the school to self-review itself, so it would do it.

You'd then say to the LEA 'what's your view of this school?' The LEA could give its view. Then I would have in three inspectors for two days. One inspector from HMI. The other two inspectors from other LEAs, so they can learn from each other, and I would invite them to write a commentary on what the school said about itself with a balance of good points and problems. It would take all of the pain away.

A Class Act

That commentary and a summary of the main report would be given to all of the parents, and if the visiting Ofsted team said 'look this is so far adrift from our impression of the school,' you would say to the school, 'you have twelve months, and at the end of twelve months you will have a full external inspection of the school,' and if you did that, you would reduce school inspections. You'd increase teacher morale massively, you'd get a better balance, you'd have a cheaper system.

Those visiting LEA inspectors would be trained by HMI, so there'd be a more consistent template across the country. You'd make sure that you had much higher and more consistent standards across the country. For my money, I am at a loss to understand why such a system isn't being introduced. It should be and it should be soon.

JZ: If we'd spoken ten years ago, the outlook for education wasn't that positive. The tone I get from you is quite positive.

TB: In 1988, I had decided to leave Oxfordshire to go and be in Keele University as I couldn't any longer lead those schools and that educational community, because I believed the national curriculum was badly designed. It was going to waste the profession away and people were going to collapse, early retirement would go up, there would be a pecking order of schools and immense damage would be done. I couldn't see further or wider. I couldn't lead, becuse what I saw I didn't like the look of. And I left, and I went into a university.

By about 1991/92, I could see how that analysis had been right, but I could also see that there was going to be a revision to the national curriculum, which there was. I was always by the way in favour of LMS, so we'd pioneered it, and I am in favour of school-based decision-making.

By 1992/93 I desperately wanted to get to an urban schooling system, because I thought we knew so much more about school improvement, so much more about teaching and learning, we could apply it and if we had political will it wouldn't matter what the government was doing, because they were hands off, so we could get on and do things.

We've got a Secretary of State and a minister now who buy that as a proposition, because they've observed what's happened, have listened have talked, want to do

A Class Act

it. I just see it as an elusive step or two away of turning the mood into one of being very very positive.

Of course you can guess where my despair lies. It lies really in the nature of Ofsted and the workings of DfEE officials.

A Class Act

5. *Who's in charge here?*

Teachers and pupils in schools today

One teacher we know recently asked us why the pupils in her class could never hear her instructions. We suggested she come out of the cupboard and face them. In this way her students might make some sense of what were otherwise a series of muffled emissions. Within this small vignette lie the salient questions relating to teachers and their charges. Do you have to like children to be a teacher? Do you have to like teachers to be a child? And when we talk of relations between the two what do we really mean? Are we leafing idly through the pages of a brightly illustrated hardbound album of *Bunty* figures, making each others' lives more fulfilling with each verb declined and every cottage-loaf baked? Or are we in reality considering a more fractious set-up of contempt and intercine warfare? Let us commence our exploration of this most fundamental relationship, by looking over our shoulder at what has gone before. By examining teacher-pupil relations in history, surely we will gain a better insight into today's school setting?

A short history of misbehaviour

It is clear that answering back and rudeness are not products of the modern age. Maybe they have been shaped and refined into living arts in recent times, but they are certainly not new phenomenon. For hundreds of years schoolchildren have been polishing and sharpening their quipping darts, in order to lob them with accuracy and sometimes venom at their tutors. Taking on a teacher is as old as time itself, and it is well known that in Adam and Eve's kindergarten (progressive in nature but not quite Montessori) the Garden of Eden echoed with the sound of Cane's whining voice insisting that he wanted to climb cherry trees, instead of participating in the prescribed nature ramble. Indeed it was this contrary nature which was to get Cane into quite a substantial pool of hot water at a later date.

As schools became more formal and children were expected to conform to a range of classroom edicts and rules, opportunities for misbehaviour multiplied. In Seventh century Spain, there was the remarkable case of Xavier Fernandez Arachio, a nine year-old studying under the spiritual but firm arm of a monastic order. His exploits included stealing all of the slates in the monastery and selling them to a street vendor in Seville, in addition to playing the lute in a 'threatening and lascivious manner' during morning prayers.

A Class Act

The monks, despairing of Xavier's ability to ever gain a decent education, reluctantly employed him in their service to invest money on behalf of the monastery, with the intention of giving any profits to local charities. Xavier rose to this challenge and in a short space of time had amassed a very tidy stockpile, but unfortunately for the order, he disappeared with the takings and set himself up as manager of a rug emporium on the Aegean coast.

In Holland, in 1352, William Goust, won infamy and excommunication from his family following an amazing stunt at the local science college he attended. Although only ten, Goust decided that a most satisfactory wheeze would be to shave off every sighting of facial hair from amongst the teaching staff.

Thus with a bristled brush and lightweight razor, he made his rounds in the stealth of an Autumn night and within half an hour, every beard and moustache clipping available had taken up residence in his knapsack. Thereafter he emptied the contents of this haul and arranged the strands into letters on the main school noticeboard which spelt 'Good Morning Oh Fresh Faced Ones.' This fiendish act earned him disfavour from the teaching fraternity, but at the same time, a small annual stipend from a local shaving foam manufacturer who was delighted with the smoothness of his operation.

In Seventeenth century France, at a fencing school in the Dordogne, purportedly for children of 'The Noble Classes.' Henri Thaillard (aged thirteen) melted each and every sabre on the school premises in the kitchen fire, in an attempt to construct a new suit of armour. On discovering the crime, the Principal, Monsieur Garton was said to have wept like a small child before he started chasing Henri through the grounds with what remained of his weapons collection.

These are but a few examples of misbehaviour on a grand scale, and such hearty exploits put the attempts of many modern day miscreants to shame. As cheekiness increased over time, and educators faced a growing swathe of insolence from their students, it seemed to many in the teaching profession, that corporal punishment was the only mechanism capable of maintaining order.

Can you feel the force?

As we have briefly witnessed, the history of classroom interaction unfolded on its fascinating course to reveal ever more boisterous and daring behaviours. When speaking calmly and reasonably did not achieve the desired effect, many pedagogues of old resorted to their fists. A huge array of striking implements came on stream in the name of classroom management. From the simple back of the hand to the ornate carved stick, all were seen as aides in the battle for setting down clear limits and instilling some degree of fear into pupils.

It was reasoned that without fear of being beaten, schools would be places where children would be free to roam without boundaries, sipping bath water or feasting on wood chippings if the fancy took them. Some educators forgot the reason they were in schools, and put aside 'Book Work' for long periods of time, to concentrate on the slipper or the cane.

When beating children was finally outlawed in this country, there was a great outcry from a small minority of the profession who had forgotten how to read and write, so busy had they been administering 'physical education' to their hostile charges. In the modern world, with beatings being illegal in the eyes of the law, it remains incredible that so many parents still pass on their children to teachers imploring them to 'hit the little swine.'

Although this prospect in some circumstances may seem very appealing, it is the teacher's duty to point out the confines of disciplinary exertion, and explain in broad brushstrokes their reliance on verbal dexterity instead of the mighty hand. This does tend to satisfy all but the most aggressive within the parental community. So, with beatings and thwackings no longer available resources to the teacher, what is the state of discipline in the modern school setting, and do the children ever do as they are told?

Shaddington Manor

Starting at the bleakest end of the behaviour continuum, it is high time for us to take a peek behind the barricades of one of those notorious institutions, which provide such anguish for education ministers and yet such unbridled pleasure for editors of tabloid newspapers. For the sake of educational advancement, and in the name of unashamed voyeurism, we shall pay a visit to Shaddington Manor - an establishment so blighted by misbehaviour that no inspector however foolhardy would ever dare step foot inside.

A government official, weighed down by the idiosyncrasies of conflicting theoretical educational models, and harassed by a superior wanting a glib phrase to describe a situation, would describe Shaddington Manor as one of our *less harmonious* schooling communities. This hapless pen-pusher would have noticed from many detailed observations and discussions, that, inside one of these 'communities' a working relationship between staff and pupils simply doesn't exist. It's not just that there are trouble spots or problem creases in a discipline model

A Class Act

waiting to be ironed out - there exists no connection whatsoever. The most that can be said is that the adults and children (or at least some of them) report to the same building each morning. Whilst the paper description 'school' implies some form of common purpose, the truth beholds two groups locked in a constant battle against each other. Whilst it would be unwise to make a sojourn at Shaddington Manor a personal priority, the necessity to undertake such an expedition has been rendered unecessary thanks to the jottings of Mr. Neville Hankin, who completed a short but eventful teaching assignment at The *Manor* and published his findings on the internet.

Neville - with seventeen years of teaching nestled under his rapidly expanding waistline, happened to notice one morning, as he was browsing through the dishevelled and spartan magazine rack in his local library, an advert for a term's contract for supply cover at Shaddington Manor. Whilst his initial reaction was to turn the page with lightening sleight of hand, something about the box-ad made him pause. He knew that Shaddington had topped the borough's 'list of fear' for as long as records had been collated. He was aware of the tarring and feathering incident not two months previously. He understood how friends and colleagues would physically attack him for even contemplating such a notion, but something within him stirred an impulsive response and he headed straight for the payphone next to the 'cookery' section.

His brief conversation with the school secretary would have been enough to put most mortals off, as the sounds of screaming and police sirens in the background made it hard to hear her directions to the place, but Neville had set his sights on a new challenge and he was undeterred

Neville's Internship

As he drove up to the metal gates the next day for his interview with the Headteacher, he was filled with romantic images from *To Sir With Love*, and felt confident that his years of experience would stand him in good stead for the days ahead. Noticing that a prison was attached to the school canteen did not even dampen his spirits. Gaining entry to the Head's office could only be achieved by walking down a series of long corridors, which were connected by iron gates, opened and closed by various subject co-ordinators. On finally reaching the Head's room, he discovered that it was only possible to address her through heat-proof glass.

She seemed very organised and forceful to Neville, and although the interview

A Class Act

lasted just nine seconds, he was reassured that he would be able to collect his timetable at the secretary's office. On collecting this document and studying its detail, Neville shrugged off the slightly worrying names given to his various classes. After all he reasoned, *The Combat Zone*, *Warrior Platoon*, and *The Nutters* could all be ironic codenames for classes of calm and sensible children. Unfortunately for Neville they were not, and the the twelve weeks he spent within the confined walls of Shaddington Manor were to be the most terrifying of his career to date.

We will not go into details concerning his classroom experiences whilst at Shaddington, for these are well documented in cyberspace, but we will note his delight at the positive aspects of his stay at Shaddington. By the end of his time there, his personal expletive dictionary had quadrupled, and he had become a skilled practitioner in several quite complex martial arts. Whilst he did move on to a permanent post at a quite genteel country school for immaculately groomed children, he did not rule out a possible return stint at some time in the future to *The Manor*.

Neville Hankin is not alone in his experience, but unlike the upbeat message he delivers about his time at Shaddington Manor, many others relive such episodes with horror and anger. They bemoan the terrible behaviour of the children in such institutions, the ridiculously low level and morale, and the pressures of daily life. Their tales should sound a jarring warning bell to anyone with any power in education.

Understanding each other is hard when you're from different planets

There is nothing quite so distasteful as seeing a teacher trying to 'get in' with children by copying their speech patterns or chosen fashion styles. But, knowing a few buzz-words and an assortment of characters means you do have a fallback position if your message is simply not getting through.

Whilst for the most part, teachers can accept that they themselves once experienced a childhood of some sort, for children it is often much harder to connect teachers to the human race. They see teachers as strange modelled figures from another planet, who descend on earth each Monday morning to impart their knowledge and skills, returning to their home galaxy on Friday afternoons to plan a few more lessons with an equally strange bunch of compatriots.

Teachers, according to many kids, have no home-life, and certainly don't watch television, go to the shops or eat. Teachers and pupils exist in a venn diagram, with

A Class Act

the shared set being schooltime. Given that a sizable portion of their time must be spent within this joint forum, it is not unreasonable to ponder what is the best approach for children to escape the censure of teachers, and how best teachers can manage children?

Excuses, Excuses

Children, at all costs, must cause as much mischief as possible without getting into trouble. This has been the mantra for generations of young people and it remains as valid today as ever. The child has a distinct advantage over the teacher in that there is only one authority figure in a classroom setting and hordes of possible wrongdoers. Thus, in a room of thirty pupils, it can be safely assumed that when a strange noise is made behind a teacher's back the teacher will have difficulty in making a correct assessment of the culprit, unless they have sophisticated surveillance equipment installed in their classroom. Children will also use their supposed naivety and salad days status, in attempting to squirm out of anything remotely challenging. It is therefore, our pleasure and privilege to introduce you to the failsafe **Homework Excuse Detector Checklist**. This handy little aide-memoire will assist anyone who works with children in ascertaining whether or not they are telling the truth pertaining to the non-appearance of a required task. The checklist does allow for that awkward and complex grey area, sometimes known as 'the truth', although it tends to err a fraction on the side of not believing anything a child ever tells you.

The Homework Excuse Detector Checklist

The Dog ate it - **Lie**, especially when there is no canine presence in the child's family.

I lost it - **Lie**, because you stuck it to their clothing with strong adhesive.

I got attacked by some kids from another school on the train and they ripped it up - **Lie**, because you've been in touch with the transport police and have received a written verification of every altercation on the travel networks.

I dropped it by accident down a drain - **Lie**, because you personally make a daily inspection of the local area's entire sewage system.

A Class Act

Some space creatures landed from another planet in a strange purple craft and took it away with them for forensic examination - **Possible Truth** as no one has yet conclusively disproved the existence of extra-terrestrial life-forms.

I didn't do it because I hate you - **Truth**, and points to be awarded for brutal honesty.

Teacher's patter

Most teachers are willing to devote some of their free time in developing a unique phraseology to deal with any signs of pupil unrest. In fact, many in the profession take no greater pleasure than from sharing one of their best turns of phrase with approving colleagues in the staffroom. And verbal magic is needed in great abundance, as children today are adroit at wheeling out a vast array of moans and whines. Stock phrases in today's arsenal include:

"I'm not doing that."

"It's not fair."

"Why ?"

These are all common responses when a child is asked to perform some very menial task like placing a pencil shaving in a dustbin..

In nine out of ten situations, any tension can be diffused simply through repetition of a command coupled with an extremely fierce and directional look.

If compliance is still not forthcoming, the well-worn phrase, "I'm not asking you, I'm TELLING you" often does the trick. If a result is still not secured then a number of other avenues can be explored.

The gentle cajoling method - "OK Adrienne I can see you're upset," can perform wonders, but can be too time-consuming and neglectful of the rest of one's charges.

The serious chat in a corner - "Right I think we need to sort this out pretty quickly, don't you? can induce reason into a child if they feel so disposed.

A Class Act

Shouting at the top of your voice with a fanatical look in your eyes and temples bulging rarely achieves anything, but does allow the teacher to let off some hissings of steam.

As a last resort sending them out, or to a higher authority - (*"That's it I've had enough"*) can be attempted. In some situations a child refuses to go to the higher authority, in which case the whole rigmarole of sending another child to fetch the Headteacher or Deputy Headteacher has to be gone through, with the rest of the class whispering frantically and getting slightly hysterical. On the other hand though, the threat of being sent to a particular person can turn a display of impudence into one of obsequious loyalty and shimmering goodness, so great is the mythology surrounding one icon residing on the school premises.

Fear me

In every school, there does always seems to be one figure to whom no child wants to be dispatched.

It may be the Head.

It may be the Deputy Head.

However, it has been widely noted that in many cases it is in fact neither of these two, but instead a senior and highly experienced member of staff whose mere name instils bowel movements in the entire school community, including those of a substantial proportion of the teaching staff. For some obscure reason, many of these custodians of remorse prefer to take lunch in their own classrooms, therefore staying out of staffroom banter and adding to the aura of mystique that surrounds them. They arrive and leave the building unseen, which leads many to deduce that they actually live somewhere on the premises, although empty gas-canisters and camping stoves found by the wheelie bins are not certain proof of this. They wear the same seasonal clothes, and like to take brisk walks in extremely cold weather. No one dares challenge them, and most can't even pluck up the courage to say 'Good morning' to them. Their 'out of hours' lives are a complete conversational taboo, although rumours about racing pigeons abound.

To see the look of abject terror on some poor kid's face when they are informed they must pay a visit to Mr. Toggle or Mrs. Falcon, is really something. It states in

A Class Act

a terrified whisper. *How could you do this to me?* It is a cruel blow to pack someone off in their direction, but mere mention of their name, even in anagram form, can work miracles.

It is of course always best to carry out all threats to their named conclusions, so if an offender does push beyond the line of tolerance, they may well find themselves treading the nervous footsteps in the direction of he or she who is to be avoided at all possible costs. Children have been known to invent rare illnesses, become ardent librarians and even take up bible studies in order to avoid having to make that journey.

The Balance of Power

Those powerful discipline demons, as mentioned above, can be called on from time to time to add some gravitas to a threat, but in reality most teachers rely on their own wits to outfox the rabble facing them. The key notion of classroom control, known as 'the balance of power' has been studied for many years and forms the backbone of a litany of teacher-training manuals.

The age old question, *how does one establish and maintain order in a class?* has never been answered satisfactorily on one side of A4.

In reality, the power balance in many classes fluctuates on a daily basis. At times, the teacher commands a steady grasp on their charges. There is a sense of goodwill, respect, and calm behaviour within the classroom, and each student feels safe and motivated. However, in other situations, the teacher has completely lost control of their pupils, and an atmosphere of smouldering anarchy invades the class.

In most classrooms in this country there is a general sense of at least some purpose, a feeling that everyone is moving in the same general direction, if not all at the same time and along exactly the same path.

Sometimes interests between staff and pupils will converge very powerfully, at the time of a great national sporting occasion, when a festival occurs or when a local news story affects the whole community.

At times such as these, the two groups can communicate on the same level, and even though their experiences are markedly different they should be able to reach some degree of understanding. If children and teachers can somehow draw out an area of agreed common purpose then they can really achieve something, like betting on the dogs or learning to write in a legible cursive script - a problem that often

A Class Act

exists for both communities.

A Class Act

6. *Don't call me colleague!*

How do teachers get on with their fellow professionals?

A grassy forecourt is illuminated by a thin shaft of light. It is early morning, and it has been raining recently. Residual droplets of water cling desperately to the window panes of the surrounding buildings. **Simmons** *hurries by, clearly in a state of some agitation. He clasps a package beneath the folds of his rumpled brown overcoat. He is in his early thirties and is wearing small oval glasses. Enter* **Ruddock** *stage right. She is forty-two, and is sporting a freshly ironed immaculate lime-green skirt-suit. She has her mind on other matters but halts abruptly when she spies* **Simmons**, *who is about to bump into her.*

Ruddock: Good morning Jeff, in a hurry today?

Simmons: *(Raising his head in surprise and stopping just short of Ruddock)* Oh, Anne, I er..I didn't see you there, you gave me a shock. Good morning, yes...good morning.

Ruddock: Why the hurry Jeff, you nearly knocked me over?

Simmons: *(Fumbling with his spectacles)* Hurry? There's no hurry, I've just got things to do, bits and pieces to tie up, you know the sort of thing.

Ruddock: Yes Jeff of course I know, I've got things of my own to take care of, but I don't take every corner like it's a sharp one at Silverstone.

Simmons: *(Getting a trifle distressed)* Look I'm sorry about that, wasn't really looking where I was going, mind on other things, I didn't actually knock into you or anything though, so I don't really see what the big deal is.

Ruddock: *(Fixing him with a hard stare)* Your being in a hurry Jeff, it hasn't got anything to do with the photocopy paper break-in?

Simmons: *(Nervously clutching the package beneath his coat and blushing)* I don't know what you're talking about, I don't know anything about any photocopy paper.

A Class Act

Ruddock: Then why the rush, why all of the embarrassment, and why the .... *(She spots the bulky item he is attempting to conceal)* Jeff, what's that under your overcoat?

Simmons: *(Backing away)* It's my... it's my wallet...anyway what have my personal possessions got to do with you?

Ruddock: *(Advancing towards the hapless figure)* Come on Jeffrey, let me have a look. It won't take a minute and I promise I won't tell anyone.

Simmons: *(Finds himself backed up against a wall)* This is ridiculous Anne, you've got no right to do this. You're being crazy, leave me alone!

Ruddock dives for his overcoat and snatches as hard as she can. **Simmons** *tries to resist, and they topple over onto the ground. He tries to contain his secret enclosure, but her extra sheen nail-polish provides her with the perfect prising weapon, and suddenly there are hundreds of sheets of photocopy paper flying unchallenged into the air. Enter* **Maddox***, stage left. She is in her late fifties and is a portly woman, wearing a tweed skirt and ocean blue chemise. On seeing the remarkable sight, she stops still, and shouts.*

Maddox: Good heavens above, if we don't have enough trouble keeping the kids in line. What on earth is going on?

Simmons *and* **Ruddock** *hastily stand up, and straighten their clothing, as* **Simmons** *tries to stuff as many sheets of paper inside his overcoat as he can manage.*

Ruddock: *(Running her fingers through her hair)* Good morning Patricia, we were just doing a bit of planning together, trying out some velocity experiments, nothing to worry about.

Maddox: *(Looking unconvinced)* Well if you say so Anne, but I think an indoor location would be a better bet for this kind of activity. I've got the mayor coming round in a minute to inspect the new water pipes.

Simmons *and* **Ruddock** *finish clearing up, and he shoots her the filthiest of filthy looks, before they part,* **Ruddock** *stage right,* **Simmons***, stage left.*

A Class Act

The baddest of bad vibes

Of course not all interactions between teachers are so dramatic, or end in an elongated position, but things can get pretty nasty out there and as the police chief in *Hill Street Blues* would always remind you, it's worth, *minding your backs.*

There are some monumental feuds that have gone on, or are being developed in many schools. These can make the most far-reaching of vendettas look like a roll-around in the safe-play area. Some people just simply don't get on, and in the world of teaching, these differences can be magnified to ridiculous proportions. Take the case of the infamous *Display Defilers* (London Borough of Havering 1993-95). These were two characters in the profession who were informed at the start of their teaching careers that their classrooms would be adjacent.

As teachers they accepted this reality with a grave nodding of heads. They realised pretty quickly though, that as humans they detested each other. Things were that bad. And they would have stayed that bad and got no worse, if they had managed to keep a lid on their simmering hostility. But days spent negotiating and intervening in pre-teen debates, left them with no patience for the adult world, and they began what was to be a campaign remarkable for both its longevity and its cunning initiative.

At first, the acts of anger were confined to minuscule things - a rubber would go missing here, a crayon would be replaced with the wrong coloured jacket there. Taken in isolation these assaults seem rather tame, but when they started to occur on a multiple daily basis, it was time for even bolder feats to take place. These took the form of fairly visual attacks: a completely destroyed display with every piece torn from the wall and smeared in indelible fluorescent green ink. A whiteboard ripped out of its brackets and smashed into a million pieces, which were then neatly stacked in a pair of training shoes.

Whilst word got round the school of this contratemps, little was done about it, as the Headteacher put it down to good old-fashioned after hours 'boisterousness.' But then things took a major turn for the worse. One of the combatants arrived in school one morning to discover a stream of water leaking from beneath his classroom door. When he turned the handle and opened it, he was fairly blown away by the cascading torrent of water which swept him up and carried him menacingly around the school grounds until he was delivered drenched and shell-shocked in a small puddle outside the secretary's office.

Worst was to come for his enemy on the following day, when he saw a bulldozer smashing through his classroom wall as he was right in the middle of drama club.

A Class Act

No one was hurt, but his room and its entire contents were reduced to a pile of discoloured rubble. It was then that the Headteacher finally stepped in, and insisted they attend a country retreat led by a leading spiritual guru on 'Inner peace and how to manage conflict in the workplace.' They only lasted seven hours because the puddings was so poor, and they escaped to the airport, got on the first available flight, and took up positions as mercenaries in the middle-east, where they became brothers in arms and the very best of friends. The school still receives the occasional postcard from them, and their legacy will naturally never be forgotten.

Whilst the lengths they went to were particularly extreme, it is not unusual for teachers to dislike each other. This can provide problems on a day-to-day basis as they are expected to sit together in countless meetings, perhaps work closely together on some aspect of the school's development and use the same facilities. Luckily though, with a large abundance of skill, and quick feet, it is able to avoid antagonists for much of one's time in school. By choosing to work in different year groups, and undertaking seperate school projects, it is possible for enemies to only ever see each other whilst waiting for the photocopier to become available, and in occasional staff meetings. If these are the only points of contact, then as long as other staff members are not drawn into side-taking, any nastiness can be reduced to the bare minimum.

Good Vibes

But wait... some teachers actually don't despise each other. In fact, in many instances the cold reserve of bitterness is not a prerequisite to being colleagues in a school. Yes, some teachers do feel positively inclined to their colleagues, and many fine friendships blossom from days spent sharing playground duty. For a start one teacher does have much in common with other teachers. You all moan a lot, you think your job is the hardest on earth and you look gleefully at the rest of the working population during half-terms. So much time is spent hunched over coffee cups and new governmental commands, that it is often hard not to form bonds of at least solidarity. There are many pathways to cross in a school career. For a start, there are those teachers who take 'parallel' classes, and may be situated very near to you on a plan of the school. There are those you prepare big projects with, such as a musical evening or a residential trip. Some share similar interests to you, and you end up taking the homework club together, or planning sporting occasions. In some cases, you simply like someone and follow the usual norms of bridge-building.

A Class Act

These friendships can develop into bonds of great significance and magnitude, and can sow the seeds of lifetime contact and warmth. As two ninety year-olds walk along the sea front in Worthing, linking arms and fashioning woolen shawls, they giggle as they recall the 'War of Melanie's elbow' and the day the packed-lunches were consumed by a local fox.

As a teacher you badly need friends within a school. There is nothing like a friendly or even half-smiling face to greet you on a dark winters morning. The warmth of a single word of support can keep your energy levels burning for hours, and the tiniest hint of praise can set one's heart dancing with pride. Of course, teachers spend so much time being or trying to be kind to children, that it is at times difficult to muster the strength to provide even the merest crumbs of comfort for your colleagues. However, that molecule of inner resolve can gently caress you to deliver a comment of delight or a squeal of approval which can make such a difference to a colleague's otherwise mundane day.

Teachers can learn a great deal from each other. They can pick up handy hints about classroom management, the best ways to utilise old egg boxes and which colours suit the skin best in autumn. Another bond is built by the realistic need for assistance. There is also a growing movement in school's for increased 'specialisation.' Teachers, after all cannot be reasonably expected to be masters of all ten school-based subjects. They have to be poor at at least one or two things, and in some cases, seven or eight. If your really weak spot is English or maths, then you're in for a hard time, but if its art or music, there are plenty of ways round it. One route is to never touch the subject. The number of teachers who *forget* whole sections of the curriculum in their haste to play to their strengths is untold. A more popular way is to to carry out 'skills exchanges' alternatively known as 'You take my class for music because you can play the piano whilst I'm tone deaf, and I'll do your science lesson.'

These are more and more regular occurrences in schools nowadays, and individuals possessing a particular ability, can find themselves if they so wish, roving around the school and teaching their particular subject to a vast range of ages. This can be highly rewarding or in some cases utterly detestable, as there is a finite amount of times you can teach children to play 'London's burning' on the recorder.

This sort of flexibility is often the bedrock of some of the country's finest schools - not finest necessarily in governmental terms, but in the manner in which they allow staff to play to their strengths and be honest about their all too obvious weaknesses. In these institutions, it is easier to form lasting friendships, because the

A Class Act

atmosphere is one of mutual co-operation instead of virulent hostility.

Romance

Believe it or not, but many of the most daring and passionate courtships in the history of romantic liaisons, have taken place amongst the steamy surrounds of old cornflake packets and industrial tubs of glue. A burgeoning love-affair between two teachers must often remain the most furtive of secrets known only to the lovers themselves and the admiring classroom displays which lovingly glance down on them. A love tryst in its infancy is a potentially savage creature when let loose on the uncontrollable tongues of a staffroom, and it is best kept private until it is on much surer footing.

If news does leak of a relationship, then it can cause all sorts of problems in a staff group. These can take the form of: *gossip, petty jealousies,* and even *verbal confrontations.*

But the truth can escape if the partners are not ingenious enough to conceal their attachment.

A stolen kiss in the science room may be witnessed by a passing cleaner as he or she adjusts his mop head before knocking and entering. A hand touched with something more than the usual fleeting reassurance can cause fascinated stares and idle comments. If the love-partners have got any sense at all, they will be completely careful, even prim, whilst in the vicinity of anything school-related, and will allow their passion to flourish in the comfort of their own homes.

Olivia Felton was a teacher who fell madly in love with another member of staff. She was intent on keeping her wondrous revelations to herself, and noted down her innermost feelings on the inside pages of a tattered old homework book. There follows, some edited highlights from her most insightful and fascinating diary.

Jan 7th:
T lent me a pencil today. Not any sort of pencil, but one that he has recently sharpened with those precise and yet gentle fingers. It was an HB, new and resplendent in its yellow and black casement. I asked for one after morning break as Lena had snapped hers over Patty's head. He reached without hesitation into his shining pencil pot and handed me the gleaming writing implement. Tomorrow I might ask for a pen.

A Class Act

Jan 22nd:
T helped me with my castles display after school tonight. I didn't even have to ask him! He was passing by and saw me weighed down under an enormous pile of childrens' artwork, and strode into my classroom. It was such an enormous gesture, as I thought I was going to be there all night. We worked for an hour and a half, stapling and sticking, while our conversation flowed freely. He steadied the ladder as I reached for the display looks magnificent, and I'm going to add the final touch - a shimering moat made from silver paper, at breaktime tomorrow morning.

Feb 17th:
Took my class on a trip today and T accompanied us. It was to be Mr. Rowbottom, but a bad case of shingles left him on his back, and you-know-who stepped in to take his place. He sat next to me on the train and even commented on how nice I looked in my tie-dyed dungarees. I tried not to blush, but felt my cheeks redden as he looked deeply into my eyes. Luckily there were no children around to see that facial exchange, but my heart beat so loudly I was convinced that someone would pull the emergency stop chord! The museum visit went extremely well, and T commended me on my planning of the trip. He said that my pre-visit had been very worthwhile, and that my worksheets were the best and most stimulating he had ever seen. He even touched my arm when making these remarks! On the journey back to school my head was in a daze of delicious fantasies, and I wasn't even phased when Melissa poured the contents of her Coke can over a besuited commuter.

March 25th:
I have been chosen to organise the summer concert, and T has volunteered to assist me. This will mean lots of late night meetings and hopefully even some contact outside of school. We looked at some sheet music together this afternoon, and he ruffled my hair playfully when I made a witty remark about Elgar! We sat on the piano school, our outer thighs pressing against each other, as he played a piece he composed for his previous school's winter play. His elegant fingers danced gracefully on the keys, as he played the hauntingly beautiful melody. I sat gazing into his profile as he gracefully made the sweetest music.

April 22nd:
We're an item! Maths planning was a mere pretence - an excuse to bring us closer together, and we kissed as T swept away my slide-rule collection and algebra games. I drove home in a whirl of passion and excitement clasping the mini-

A Class Act

calculator pen he gave me close to my chest. I can't believe it's actually happened, and want to shout out my good fortune to the whole world, but we have agreed to keep it a secret, at least for the time being.

May 5th:
One of the noisier children in **T's** class saw us talking together this morning and asked us if we were 'special friends.' We told him to leave us alone and return to his bouncy-ball which he dutifully did. We reaffirmed the need for utmost secrecy, as it could prove disastrous if the rest of the staff got wind of our love. We have decided to act less informally towards each other around the school, and where possible to avoid any physical contact, even shoulder patting. We have also agreed to recruit some other members of staff to help us with the musical evening, to avoid the starting of any wickedly lashing tongues.

May 20th:
Unable to control our desires, we stole a kiss by the music system in the hall today, but were disturbed by the clanking of the caretaker's milk trolley. Seperating immediately, **T** immersed himself in a musical instruments brochure, whilst I performed some country dancing steps. Due to the caretaker's complete obsession with his trolley, we completely evaded any suspicions, and even managed to laugh about the incident. I feel it is nearing a point from which there is no public return.

May 27th:
T grabbed my waist this morning and gave me an enormous cuddle just after I had dismissed my class for lunch. I playfully reprimanded him whilst thrilling in the heat and masculinity of his embrace. Just as we were parting, Will, the English co-ordinator strode into my classroom, and stopped in his tracks as if he was interrupting some unknown liason. I straightened my hair, and said a quick and formal goodbye to **T**, whilst dealing with Will's enquiry about the missing magnetic letter board.

June 10th:
T and I announced our engagement this morning to a stunned staffroom. Mr. Patkins dropped a science catalogue into the bowl of *Quaker Oats* he eats each morning, and Heather Sampson started crying. Everyone gave us a rapturous round of applause, and we informed them that although the wedding will be small, they will all be invited. Everyone accepted this invitation most graciously, and all of the

A Class Act

clothes catalogues have been wheeled out in the rush to purchase the most glittering outfit. T and I cannot keep our eyes from each other, and the talk in school has been of nothing else today. I feel ensconced in a warm glow, the like of which I have never felt, save for the time I got a distinction on my *technology with the under-fives* course.

****

Whilst Olivia Felton's passions make for lively reading and a dramatic backdrop for the rest of her colleagues, most schools are sadly bereft of such drama. In fact, the most exciting most schools get, is the regular weekly staff-meetings that every school forces upon its citizens.

Staff meetings

Staff meetings generally take two forms. The first is known as an INSET meeting (in-service educational training), whereby an outside speaker or a member of staff will enlighten everyone about the wonders of maths taught through freemasonry, or the benefits of the latest reading scheme which has no pictures or words, but costs one hundred and forty nine pounds ninety-nine.

These meetings can at times (although it is very rare) be awesome happenings, where a dynamic individual can present a breathtaking spectacle which will open everyones' eyes to some marvellous teaching technique or hidden resource. For example, one incredibly enthusiastic music teacher took a staff group of utterly reluctant singers and turned them into a glistening performing troupe, complete with three-part harmonies and frilled collars. So passionate was their newfound love of song, that they insisted on cutting a CD of their own tunes, which bubbled under the classical top one hundred for several weeks. They performed not only in their own town, but all over the country, and got such a good name for themselves that some were able to leave their teaching careers altogether.

In another example of the fantastic INSET offering, a history co-ordinator actually managed to convince his colleagues that they had travelled back in time to Shakespeare's Stratford - the only problem being that when he announced the session was over, they refused to speak in a modern tongue, and took some persuading that they had returned to the present.

However, for the most part these supposedly informative and stimulating meetings range from just about tolerable to achingly dull. Whilst many see this as

A Class Act

the most cumbersome of burdens to bear each week, others use the time for furtive pursuits whilst giving an air of healthy interest. Thus, hundreds of items of clothes have been knitted during staff meetings, thousands of letters to dear ones have been composed, and one woman in Plymouth managed to complete her doctoral thesis on *Womens' bodices and osteopathy 1670-1830*, during the Wednesday afternoon gatherings in her staffroom.

Some of those who present these meetings simply hand out a document and read through it - an activity which is bound to drive most people to fury and tedium bordering on insanity. The more skilled presentation experts produce overheads, slide-shows and multi-media presentations to keep interest alive and their listeners awake. After all, there is nothing worse after a hard day in the classroom than listening to someone talking drivel at you, the main point of which you could have grasped by reading a fifteen-word sentence in as many seconds.

The second type of staff meeting is more of a general policy/discussion forum. During these, anything relating to school life is allowed to be discussed from broken urinals to scandals in the local political hierarchy. The minutes of such a meeting is included to give a flavour as to the breadth of what goes on. It is from a a large three-form entry school in Canterbury. These minutes were scrawled in such an inpenetrable handwriting style that an expert was drafted in to decode the spindly letters and make some sense of it all, but we are able to present in full the complete log of this particular session.

Staff Meeting.
Wednesday 23rd.
3.45 p.m.
Present: Everyone except for Gillian.

Apologies: Gillian sent a note about her ear re-shaping appointment, which was accepted whilst several members of staff asked for the contact number.

Minutes from last meeting couldn't be located, so we had to wake Clive to go and look for them. He was unable to find them, so they were agreed anyway.

<u>**Items:**</u>

1. Name-calling: Been noted that the phrase *Egghead* is doing the rounds and this is sometimes prefaced with *Ugly* - a pastime that is causing distress to some of the

A Class Act

younger children. Agreed that Susan, Headteacher, will do an assembly on eggs, demonstrating that their form is wholly dissimilar to the human head. Hopefully this will stop the verbal silliness.

2. Discussion about introduction of houses and house points into the school: Got quite heated, and Angela cried. Possible house names are:

i) *Types of fish* (Cod, Halibut, Pike and Roe).

ii) *Salads* (Caesar, Three Bean, Mixed and Potato).

iii) *Terms connected with waste disposal* (Rubbish, Binliners, Processing Plant and Refuse).

iv) *Colours from a D.I.Y warehouse catalogue* (Milky Green, Flouncing Yellow, Refrigeration Blue and Zestful Pink).

Simon suggested *types of tree* (Oak, Ash, Sycamore and Willow), but was shouted down for being ridiculous. The choice will be put to the kids, but we'll ignore what they say and make our own minds up.

3. Litter Patrol: It was felt that too much litter was being discarded in the playground, and Stephanie the art co-ordinator has volunteered to make a mobile out of it all. This will spell out the words 'Litter is bad for your health and looks offensive' and will be hung at the entrance to the hall.

4. Theatre company visit: Following last year's highly successful *Wizard in Silky Stockings* show, The Abominiable Cheese-Grater Theatre In Education Company have offered to put on their latest production *The Wine-Gum Mystery*, at a reduced cost of one pound fifty per child. In spite of the massive volume of complaints we received last time, we've stuck out our necks and booked them again.

5. Open evening: There will be no open evening this term, as no one can face it. Instead a parents v staff pub quiz evening has been organised and Richard is supplying some unusual foreign beers.

6. Playground duty: Been problems with this as some staff are sloping off early to

A Class Act

grab a coffee before they have to ring the bell, thus leaving the playground unattended. Compromise reached is that a machine will be installed in the playground to provide coffee, tea and synthetically powdered Bovril to stem the inclination to desert.

7. Pay slips: Dina, Deputy Head, noted that people had been opening other peoples' pay slips and laughing publicly at their pitiful salaries. This has caused bad feeling and a sense of mistrust, particularly as one particularly computer literate member of staff has started using school computers to hack into colleagues' bank accounts. Deputy said all slips will be handed directly to staff, and any reported wrongdoings will be placed in the hands of the local constabulary.

8. Marking: Colin, assessment co-ordinator, had a gripe about the poor standards of marking at the top of the school. He said several teachers have been marking whilst carrying out completely different activities, like holding a dinner party or playing tennis. He asked for all books to be handed to him for scrutiny. Elsa tried to rebel against this, but the rest reluctantly agreed to go along with the request.

9. Biscuit sale: Helen reported that the sale had been a great success and had raised seven pounds and thirty pence, which had been used to cover the ingredients. The Danish shortbread that Hazel made was very tasty, but its tough texture broke several teeth and there is talk of legal liability.

10. Poachers: Susan told meeting that a couple of poachers had been spotted on the school grounds following the rumoured sightings of grouse in the vicinity. Some children had been offered small sums of money to carry nets around behind the poachers in the hope of capturing some of the birds. Mike, caretaker, shouted at the men and shook his fists, but they laughed at him. We agreed to keep an eye out for them, and to pocket any cash offered to the children.

11. Assemblies: Staff put this matter very delicately to Susan, as she can be very sensitive. It was generally felt that assemblies were going on for too long, and that they had to be shortened. Tuesday's lasted two and a half hours and was about Susan's trip to Canada last summer. Children tried to stick with it, but got pretty fidgety after the first ten minutes. Susan has promised to restrict future ones to twenty minutes, although we agreed the matter would be reviewed at half-term.

A Class Act

12. Staff Fridge: Complaints have been made about Alfred's use of the staff fridge which is intended for food and drink. He's been using it for storing all of his experimental glues for the woodwork course he's attending. This would be fine, but several members of staff are finding their sandwiches inextricably linked to coke cans, and Helen's Kit-Kat (which she likes to eat when its cold and brittle) was moulded to a tupperware of Colin's tuna salad this lunchtime. Alfred agreed to find other accommodation for his glues, but seemed a little hurt.

A.O.B (any other business): Head thanked everyone for their attendance at the Elizabethan barndance and meeting was called to a close. Two members of staff suffered minor injuries in the rush for the door.

Thus a whole avenue of points and issues is explored in your average discussive staff meeting. There is an element of truancy relating to these after school treats, and some folk are noticeably absent from every one, hoping that if they stick to this pattern they will remain undetected. This is not the case, and those who stay away must often face the cold commands of the Head or Deputy who corner them as they are loading their car with a box of books for marking.

However, most teachers will only miss the odd session because in reality, whatever the boredom quotient, there will be some slices of interest or gossip that may be just too tasty to miss. It is also true, that when one misses a staff meeting, one becomes acutely aware of the knowing looks passing round a staffroom the next morning, and one realises one's own inadequacy when the latest policy initiative has been misunderstood.

As a rule it is better to sit through some of these interest-free zones, for that one piece of information or guidance which can be of great benefit to the individual.

In many schools, to ensure a full attendance there is a time limit on staff meetings, so that everyone knows when they can go home, and how long their nap can stretch to. This tends to work very well, although the school who placed this limit at four minutes, found that they had problems resolving any disputes or getting any policies formulated.

So, what of the question, can teachers get on with each other? Our answer is compartmentalised into a resounding YES, a shrill NO, and a timid MAYBE. Schools can be domains of passionate love or gnawing hate. Lifelong patterns of positivity or negativity can be set in motion within their confines. Greta emotional journeys take place within classrooms and corridors. Of course, it is far better to have a school where everyone gets on with each other in a calm good-natured

A Class Act

environment, but if the truth be told, a little tension can add a dash of colour to what might otherwise be a fairly grey world.

A Class Act

7. Captain, you're wanted on the bridge

Meet your management team and Governors

For your average school teacher, a day's work involves a great deal of decision-making and diplomacy. With thirty or so children to take care of, each day is bound to bring forth new demands and challenges. But what happens when the chips are really down, and something serious needs to be addressed? It is high time to pass on the torch of responsibility to its rightful owners.

Headteachers

However hassled anyone else in a school may be. However downtrodden and exhausted. However dishevelled and morose. There is always someone who is more stressed. In the majority of schools this is the job description of the Headteacher, whose role changes overwhelmingly as each academic year passes and fades. Whilst in the 'old days' hordes of youthful entrants to the profession cited Headship as their ultimate goal, nowadays death is mentioned as a preferable alternative.

There was a time when a Headteacher's office was holy territory, unpenetrable for all except the most servile of pupils or the most obsequious parents. This steel-enforced security mesh has been gradually untangled by a public literally forcing themselves and their increasing demands towards the centre of this inner sanctum. Gone is the slightly distant, old-fashioned caricature, who was able to spend their days pacing corridors looking for unclean children to berate.

The modern Headteacher has to be something of a marketing and PR guru if he or she wants to cut the mustard. Presentation is a huge part of the job as the public face of the school seems to be everyone's property in the modern age.

Today's Headteacher is a manager more than a teacher, and contact with children is often limited to assemblies or lectures on the wrongs of hitting people with dustbins. Of course, some are able to juggle the heavy demands placed upon them, and do spend some time back in the classroom, perhaps even conducting a little bit of teaching. But, for the most part, the Headteacher's day is made up of:

reprimands.
phonecalls. and letter-writing.
meetings of a thousand kinds.
liaising with other organisations.

A Class Act

The good Head must be totally efficient in two fields;

1) Delegation

2) Deflection

By **delegation**, we mean giving tasks to other people that the Headteacher does not wish to do. For example, dealing with a particularly troublesome parent, or pointing out to a newly qualified teacher that crampons are not appropriate footwear for P.E. lessons. Some Heads take the principle of delegation to its logical limit, and leave themselves with nothing to do other than play with the various confiscated hand-held computer games that end up on their desks.

By **deflection**, we refer to that fine skill of bouncing away accusations aimed at oneself and laying the blame at somebody else's door. For instance, when an Ofsted inspector questions the need for teaching how to fish in fresh water streams, within a curriculum module on 'aviation,' a sensible Head will deftly point the enquirer in the direction of the geography co-ordinator, whilst slipping out behind the building and driving home at great speed.

If a Headteacher can manage to excel in both of these areas, then their day-to-day existence will not be eked out in a pool of dread and sweatily-delivered excuses. If they cannot hit these organisational heights, then a cheesy lifestyle will be forced upon them simply by the nature of the hostile forces that habitually surround them. Let's face it, a Headteacher has got the teaching staff, the parents, the kids, the education authority, the government, the community, the local papers and a wide range of assorted busybodies on their case, all the time, and all demanding precious fragments of energy and committment. It is, therefore, not surprising, that some Headteachers set aside a period of time each day, during which they refuse to have contact with any other humans. Some use this space for quiet reflection or tai-chi, whilst others practice swift jerking movements with a slingshot and a bag of pebbles.

Many older Headteachers state quite openly that if they were faced with the prospect of beginning their job in the modern age, they would opt for early retirement instead, even if they were only in their mid-twenties. The amount of paperwork they are expected to complete is reason enough to balk at the prospect of a Headship. The reams of endless forms to deal with, makes digging holes and filling them in again seem like a worthwhile pursuit.

And yet, some in the teaching profession are still lured by the frothing chalice,

A Class Act

and apply for Headteacher jobs, even accepting them when they pass the interview. These people must be either commended or consoled, but whatever the case, an infinitely tough personality and excellent non-verbal talents are essential for the job. So that when someone needs to be told to be silent, an eyebrow raised a micrometre will do the trick. It should also be pointed out to any soul harbouuring aspirations of rising to the zenith of the teaching ladder, that the job of Headteacher has been very much professionalised, and whereas in the good old days it was alright to just apply for a post and get it on merit, now courses have to be attended, qualifications attained, and allegiances sworn. It is a road littered with heavy obstacles and fallen lumps of foliage. We wish anyone who is going that way the warmest of best wishes, and remind them to have a very detailed map, and a sizable flask.

Deputy Headteachers

The Deputy Headteacher is the right-hand woman or man to the Headteacher, and can lead three completely different existences.

Model A) Enjoys a brilliant rapport with the Head that borders on friendship, although both back away when ever hot chocolate is served instead of tea. The Deputy Headteacher, with the Headteacher, forms an extremely solid and powerful bloc within the school, and they achieve their aims relatively easily, by providing a united front and a close behind the scenes working liaison. First-name terms are always applied and laughter is not an uncommon activity.

Model B) Enjoys a relatively decent relationship with the Headteacher, but has several major policy differences, and they disagree politely on a number of committees. The Headteacher tends to win these little battles of will, although any strain of success experienced by the Deputy Headteacher is enjoyed by voyeuristic onlookers. First-name terms are usually applied, although formal terms are used in front of others. Smiles pass between the two and kind words are exchanged from time to time.

Model C) Detests the Headteacher and is loathed in return. Barely on speaking terms and tries to form a wedge between the staff and Headteacher. Will go to remarkable lengths to achieve stated goals, including calling major strike action, setting up picket lines within the school grounds, and holding benefit concerts for

A Class Act

the strikers' families in the nursery's wendy house. Can hardly utter each others' names, and when forced to do so, hiss them out with anger and seething rivalry. Can't face any eye-contact but when face to face, scowl at each other like the competitors in an illegal dog-fight.

Whichever model is applicable, the Deputy Headteacher does generally have a foot in both camps, because whilst she is supposedly 'in' with the Head, she is also usually a class teacher and thus a part of the staff-room camaraderie (if morale permits its continued existence). It can be a very difficult line to tread, and some Deputies have problems balancing their roles, sometimes ending up actually telling themselves off, whilst the rest of the staff stare at them with frightened expressions shadowing their faces.

Deputy Headteachers are not always just taking a nap on the way to waking up to the challenges of Headship. Some stay at the job for years, preferring the dual-role to any ascension to the number one post, and leave the profession having never been addressed as 'Headteacher.' Some wish for the move upstairs, but never quite make it, and this can lead to years of bitterness and the making of voodoo dolls. Some do make the break, and take on the full mantle of a school, be it their present one or a new pature.

The Head and the Deputy often form part of what is known as a school's 'management team', and the other component of this cabal are the senior teachers.

Senior Teachers

Senior teachers are known as such, either by dint of longevity in the job, or a specialism in a particular area of the curriculum. Thus Mildred Timpernell (37 years teaching experience) is recognised as a senior teacher, despite the fact that she has consistently refused to keep up with any developements in the national curriculum and still teaches a daily weaving lesson on her handmade loom, as is Sherrie Huston (3 years qualified) who possesses specialist knowledge of maths and in particular the use of the abacus in everyday life. Both Mildred and Sherrie are part of their respective school's management teams - bodies which meet weekly to discuss the weighty issues of the day, and attempt to undertake some important decisions in the name of the school.

Senior teachers often take responsibility for certain areas of school life, be it a particular age range of children, supervising the assessment or record-keeping procedures, or overlooking all issues relating to tarmac on the school premises.

A Class Act

Their initiatives and findings are then brought back to the management team for acceptance or derision. It is fascinating to note in relation to school management teams, the proliferation of business and management terms into the school lexicon. Phrases like *developement plan*, *target setting* and *performance indicators* are all borrowed from the business world. Whilst there is nothing wrong in trying to instill efficiency and sound planning into schools, it must never be forgotten that the average business doesn't have a few hundred unpredictable children marauding over their premises each day, and thus some terms from the world of the sharply-dressed executive may not be totally appropriate to educational settings.

If a management team, and ultimately the Headteacher and Deputy Headteacher carry the can for any school, there is yet another body which burdens a great weight of responsibility and is open to the continual spotlight of scrutiny.

The Governors

Every school has to have a governing body. The governors are legally responsible for the school, and are elected from political parties, the parental community, the local populace and from amongst the teachers. This last faction are usually there to defend their own interests and fight off the pushier parental elements who desire all-night open evenings and accelerated learning for foetuses. The governing body generally meets once every half-term, although in a time of crisis more frequent meetings may be required. The Headteacher and/or the Deputy Headteacher generally attend these meetings, and unless an agenda item is highly sensitive, the meetings are open to anyone connected with the school.

The Chair of the governing body is often a local councillor or an active member of the local community. Their brief is to conduct all of the meetings in an appropriately solemn manner and to lead the body in the direction of efficient and reasonable judgements. This can work very well, but there are of course individuals who view the post as a way of caressing their own egos and throwing some of their directional clout around.

Take the case of Mrs. Rumford, a Tunbridge Wells business woman in her early forties who became the Chair of her local school's governing body after a three-way battle with a Labour councillor and a neuro-scientist. She imposed the strictest discipline on her governing body and actually sent out three-line whips on a regular basis to boost attendance. She became very dictatorial and was known to hold some of the most important sessions in the staff toilet, which could only accomodate one person, and thus she was freed from the burden of having to partake in any form of

A Class Act

democratic voting. Her reign of terror was eventually curtailed by a bloodless coup, in which all of the other governors met secretly in a local wine-bar and voted her out of office. She was oblivious to this decision for many months, and continued with her 'public convenience' meetings, blissfully unaware that the real decision-making process was going on far away.

The governors of a school are supposed to be a group of sensible responsible citizens who have the interests of the children at heart and who've been selected because they are seen in some way as being capable of making wise and mature decisions. Whilst this is crystal clear in theory, the reality is often a little cloudier. At times, it is hard to fill all o the positions on a governing body, and word may go out that applicants are required. Adverts are sometimes placed in the local press, and one Chair of a governing body even went on local a T.V station to plead for new members. When this process does take place, prospective governors are asked to apply by letter, stating why they wish to be appointed and what they might be able to contribute. When these letters eventually arrive on a school's premises, the present governing body members sit round a large table in the staffroom talking in serious tones about the nature of the applications and ruminating over who should be invited for an interview. Many of the applicants make reasonable and appropriate candidates, but as we show below, some of those who write in stand little chance of ever making it.

Dave Flaxton from Liverpool wrote this letter to his local school's Chair of governors when he saw an insert in his local paper.

Dear sir/madam,

As a local window-cleaner, I can see a marvellous opportunity that lies within your school and I would therefore like to be considered for the post of governor. With so much glass on your premises, the dust and the childrens' spitting must make the place look awfuly shabby. At 50p a window, I could provide an excellent and reliable service and still have time to come and chat to you in the evenings. I am in a position to offer a special cut-price deal to the other governors and I also provide a car valeting service.

Best wishes

David Flaxton.

A Class Act

David's application was unsuccessful as was that of Patricia Duncan from Hampshire who also wrote a well-meaning letter.

Dear Sir/Madam,

I am a retired book-keeper and I live five minutes away from your grounds. I was actually in the first ever reception class at the school and still have fond memories of the glass of milk and crumbly biscuits we used to eat whilst resting in our hammocks. I have a wealth of experience in dealing with figures and sums, and I would dearly like to become aquainted with your school budget and its intricacies. Do not be put off by my lengthy criminal record for fraud and embezzlement - these were all offences that took place in different parts of the country, and thus my reputation in this area is untarnished. Looking forward to hearing from you.

Mrs. R. Duncan.

Ian Gentleman from Guildford was actually invited for an interview on the strength of the following letter, but five minutes spent in his company was enough to dissuade the panel of his appropriateness for the task.

Dear Madam Chairwoman,

How exciting that a place is available on your governing body - a body which I might add, has a reputation for being run in the smoothest and most orderly fashion. Let me tell you a little bit about myself. I am what is known as 'a professional committee buff.' I am at present on seventeen committees, from the local church army to the trades association for leather boot manafacturers. Being so well versed in the art of committee practice and procedure, I feel sure that I would be able to make a serious contribution to the workings of your group, and would even like to volunteer myself as minute-taker, because I am the treasurer of the new library minute-takers foundation. I can do 60 words per minute shorthand, and in my spare time I enjoy golf and collecting old pickle jars.

Ian.

It can therefore be said in all earnestness that a vast cross-section of our society

A Class Act

shows an interest in becoming a governor of their local school. Whilst for some it is an act of political or societal ambition, for others it is simply because they care about their childrens' future, and want to have a say in the direction their school takes. Of course some governing bodies are run brilliantly and meetings last about an hour, with waffle and anecdotes cut down to a bare minimum. It is the ones which relish all-night sittings and great meaningless debates that must be avoided if one wishes to maintain one's sanity.

A Class Act

8. Interview with Doug McAvoy

The NUT has often been viewed as a very militant union, and Doug McAvoy as an outspoken adversary of government. The NUT annual conference created a storm several years ago, when David Blunkett was jostled by a group of angry teachers. McAvoy doesn't pull his punches and has a reputation for straight-talking. He has stated on many occasions his committment to modernise and democratise the NUT, and to drag it away from the divisions caused by noisy entryist factions. When he phoned us, we expected nothing less than a no-holds-barred account of teachers' struggles against the short-termism of successive governments. We weren't disappointed.

Doug McAvoy's early teaching career took place in Newcastle secondary schools where he taught P.E, in addition to maths and science. Subsequently he lectured in maths at Newcastle College of Art and Technology. He became a member of the NUT executive in 1970. He took up appointment as Deputy General Secretary of the NUT in February 1975. In 1989, he became the first elected General Secretary in the union's 120 year history. He was re-elected to that post in 1994. He is also President of the European Trade Union Committee for Education.

JZ: It seems that we're getting mixed messages from new Labour. On the one hand we're getting a lot of praise for teachers, but on the other there's condemnation. Are you seeing the same sort of mixed message?

DM: Yes and I'm not surprised. When they were first elected, among their first statements was that there would be a sort of stick and carrot approach. That there would be pressure and support. I think what teachers have experienced to date is more of the pressure than the support. So I'm not surprised at what we're getting, that doesn't mean to say I'm not disappointed by it. I can understand politically why they may wish to be seen trying to improve educational standards. That's a political agenda for them with their electorate, having made education their priority they want to present to the public a government that is 'making a difference' as the Prime Minister would say. I think the balance of the pressure and support has been wrong. There ought to have been much more support from the very beginning, and the pressure ought to have been less, and certainly less public.

JZ: They say they're new, but they've adopted some of the posturing and some of

A Class Act

the policies of previous Conservative administrations, for instance in being very prescriptive with something like the literacy hour, and the numeracy hour. Do you share that analysis?

DM: Yes, I think their newness is new Labour and not new government. We have put out material which has talked of new Labour, old Tory. Some of the decisions they have taken, some of the statements they have made and certainly the emphasis behind some of the approach they've adopted has been similar to, if not identical with the kind of approach we've had over the years from the Conservative government. Indeed ironically that approach was probably softening on the part of the Tories particularly during the Gillian Shepherd regime, because I think they judged that they probably needed to try to re-establish themselves with education and with teachers.

If you get a new government that's determined with not being charged as going soft on teachers and education, then I suppose they start from the point that the others left off and don't lessen the attack, and the naming of shaming of schools was an example of that. I don't think the Tories would have ever done that. The staging that was imposed by new Labour was a more restrictive staging than had ever been applied by the Tories. You can go on and find more examples, you've quoted some curricular examples where the prescription was the same. I suppose you have to set against that their decision on the primary curriculum, freeing up, and it would seem giving more flexibility to schools and to teachers.

Our concern about that of course, is that you free up the curriculum in one statement, but because you put so much emphasis on numeracy and literacy, and you continue to apply and develop league tables, based primarily on subject areas, then you make it difficult for teachers to respond to the needs of their pupils in the most flexible ways. Because they've got to keep their eye on the main measure of performance, that measure of performance being jointly, numeracy and literacy.

JZ: If we could move to teachers' pay for a moment, the new proposed threshold for pay. Isn't this just a way of saying that we can't give all teachers suitable and substantial increases?

DM: I think that's the financial consequence of the approach. Their presentation is different of course. Their presentation is about seeking to pay those who are good,

A Class Act

and therefore reward performance. But the minute you start to ration the amount of the reward, I don't mean for each individual, I mean the amount available for rewards, you lose that argument.

We've been able to show that some two hundred and fifty thousand teachers are currently trapped at point nine of the scale, and the government now admits that a significant minority will not be able to go across the threshold. One of the reasons for that, is that one of the tests for deciding whether or not a person crosses the threshold is whether or not the school's budget will allow it. So in a sense, the justification for a sort of cynical view that you create two categories of teacher, so that you can pay one more, and one less, so that you don't have to pay them all more, is proven.

JZ: In terms of the teaching unions and the NUT in particular, is there an argument for saying that these organisations have lost the media battle over the last few years. In the hearts and minds of the public, the perception of teachers has changed so much. Have the unions been too reactive and not pro-active enough?

DM: I think undoubtedly the area where we've had greatest difficulty is countering the criticisms of teachers and schools. There's nothing new in that mind. That didn't start with he Tories. You go back to Jim Callaghan as Prime Minister, and the great debate. Now that was done for exactly the same purpose as the most recent attacks. The purpose of that was to persuade the public that all was not well in our schools, and that therefore, there had to be greater questioning of the performance of teachers. That great debate took place at a time when there was a very real shortage of teachers emerging and there was a real need for a massive injection into pay.

The Callaghan government decided the best way to avoid that or oppose that, was to seek to discredit the profession, and the work teachers were doing. That was continued by the Tories. If they hadn't discredited schools they couldn't have argued for the quite significant changes that came with the 1988 Education Act, they couldn't have made sure they were able to take away negotiating rights. And likewise with Labour, unless you can persuade the public that there's something wrong, you can't persuade the public that you should change. So, that has been a very important propaganda area for government over a long time, and government controls the media, and the unions can't break into that.

A Class Act

However much we promote the good things, the work that teachers do and the quality of that work, more and more teachers are presented by the media as either being carping or 'they're bound to say this,' and also balanced against criticism from people like the government and the Chief Inspector. Now when you say have we lost the script, I think we haven't been able to defeat government on that issue. I think we have been able to pull issues back at times, both with the Tories and more particularly with Labour, making sure that parents in particular rather than the public generally, as well as teachers, because some teachers need to be reminded, are aware of the things that have to be done on the support side if you're going to be able to deliver any of the improvements in levels of achievement from a pressure side. I think that has worked.

The amount of money being injected into education is in part the result of that, the Secretary of State would claim that the green paper is in part due to that kind of pressure. The attitude of parents in the localities is still one of a belief in education, and belief that the teachers in the schools are doing a good job. Though the national response might not show that, once you talk to people in the locality of a group of schools, their attitude changes. So I think we've clung on, probably as best as we could, against the onslaught and the media control, but undoubtedly they've gained more than we've been able to counter.

JZ: What about the NUT's reputation for possessing that militant element? There was a lot of press when David Blunkett was jostled at an NUT conference. It seems that some members had a disproportionate voice to their numbers. Do you think this has changed?

DM: The decision-making processes in the union have changed. We've embarked more and more with full consultation of all members. We've done it over bureaucracy. We're currently doing it over the green paper. We did so on alternative pay structures. The response we get from members through the consultation exercise is valuable, because it does demonstrate a difference of view from the active member who becomes a local association officer.

Sadly, within the union, I think there has been the development of political factions and political groups, who operate in part on the whim of the political group of their members. That has been bad for the union over about twenty years, it's been developing for that length of time. It was particularly apparent in the mid-eighties,

A Class Act

when there was a protracted action with government, and the way in which the union became divided over a potential settlement, history will show that had we been in support of that settlement, we would have had an agreement that would have stood us in very good stead over the last ten or twelve years. That wasn't to be.

I think also the decisions of conference from time to time, and this is given great publicity by the media, are then not supported by when they're put to the test by members. So we do have, on occasion, a publicity that is generated which is not the NUT. The best way to counter that is by having the type of consultation that we embark upon.

JZ: Can I ask you about the NUT's call for one union? Would this not make one huge and unwieldy body which would react more slowly to events, because of its sheer size. I mean balloting nearly half a million people would surely be a very lengthy process?

DM: I don't think that would necessarily be the result, and even if it was, I don't think the disadvantages that come with size outweigh the advantages that come with unity and size. What we would be creating would be a single voice for the profession. I think that's vital in terms of the circumstances teachers and schools will face in the foreseeable future. We will be removing the competition between the existing organisations, which is costly, and as a result of that, more money would be invested in the services for teachers, or it would cost teachers less to get the services they get now.

I think the size factor can be overcome by structures which ensure the full participation of members. In order to get teachers to participate fully in an organisation, you have to lessen the extent to which that participation has to be, through attending a meeting of an association or a branch. You've got to make more readily available means of consultation. Technology allows us to do that, in a way that doesn't necessarily take up a long time, by using web sites and the internet. It wouldn't be difficult to get groups of teachers together at lunch time and get them to discuss something among themselves and respond.

I think the value of one organisation being able to speak for four hundred and eighty thousand, half a million teachers, and say that's the voice of the profession, would outweigh any disadvantages. The green paper exercise is I think the most appropriate example of that. The government claims to have had something like ten or twelve thousand replies to its consultation exercise. We carried out our own in the union. We've currently got thirteen thousand and I've no doubt the twelve thousand the government has would include local authorities, would include parents, would include business, all kinds of people who picked up one of these response forms and have pushed it back. What would be valuable for teachers is if the profession could speak as one voice in response to the green paper. If the profession could do that, then the opportunities for the government to impose changes would be seriously reduced, but I think unfortunately the unity isn't there for that to be used in protection of teachers at the minute. But I think if it had been there then we would have been able to use it to our advantage.

JZ: In terms of schools in disadvantaged areas, what could the NUT be doing more for teachers in these schools?

DM: Well I think we can be campaigning with government to change the funding mechanism. I think the funding mechanism now doesn't allow the local authority to pump sufficient, additional resources in. The fair funding formula won't change that. I think that was a mistake, that Labour didn't move more quickly to a more radical change in the funding mechanism or promise us a further review.

I think we could give more support directly to teachers in those schools through not only the resources that come from government, through local education authorities, but in some of the material that's produced in order to help them do their job. I think in the sense of the education action zones, there's nothing wrong with the education action zones, providing it's contained within the local education authority, and not put out to business, and provided then, that the resources that are put in are not to the cost of the schools that are outside the zone. So we could use the concept of the zones to give the necessary support. But giving the schools more money won't necessarily turn those schools round. It won't make the change that needs to be made. You need to put many more resources, better staffing ratios, better provision generally, more non-teaching support, so you could make a real impact in those schools.

JZ: In terms of Ofsted, if we could start off with Christopher Woodhead himself. Surely, Mr. Woodhead is promoting himself to such an extent that one actually

A Class Act

forgets about the organisation he fronts. Staking up controversy and his own personal profile?

DM: I think there's an element of that. Recently Chris Woodhead and indeed the Secretary of State defended his rather large increase in pay on the grounds that he was the education regulator for government, and therefore that his pay ought to be the same as the regulators for gas and for electricity, and other commodities. Now I think your point is proven if we were to ask teachers of the public, name the regulator for gas. Name the regulator for electricity. They wouldn't be able to do so, because they see their role as one that regulates a service and how best they can maintain the regulation of that service.

I think that's the way the Chief Inspector ought to be operating. He ought to be advising government. This Chief Inspector has determined that he will operate differently from early days I think, with the support from the Tory party when it was in government, and with the support of the Labour government. For them it's quite refreshing to have someone who's seemingly independent, with a whole team of inspectors reporting to him, who condemns schools and condemns teachers.

JZ: Are Mr. Woodhead's comments about staff-pupil relationships a resigning issue? (*Christopher Woodhead when addressing a conference at Exeter University stated that staff-pupil relationships could be 'educative' and 'experiential' -* JZ/DP).

DM: No I don't think so. I've been asked should he be sacked. I don't think he should be sacked. I think he should have been sacked for the way in which he has abused his position as Chief Inspector. I think he should have been sacked because he has been biased in his reporting about teachers and schools. And if he wasn't sacked, he should never have had his contract renewed. They're reasons about how he fulfils the job he's employed to do. I question whether he should have answered in the way he did, and I'm not certain he ought to stray outside of the role of Chief Inspector. Undoubtedly, there's scope there for reprimand, but I don't think for sacking.

JZ: What about this figure of fifteen thousand failing teachers? Chris Woodhead said that he made this figure initially based on a theoretical model, but in his next annual report says he will provide 'firm evidence' that fifteen thousand is the

A Class Act

correct figure. (*The report did highlight the figure of fifteen thousand, once again stirring up much controversy - JZ/DP*). What do you make of that figure, and what would you place the figure at, if it's possible to do?

DM: No, I don't think it's possible to do. I think the figure that he gives is widely off the mark, and indeed he was quoting fifteen thousand, and not only did he quote a figure, he said that they should be sacked. I think when he publishes the new figures, he'll not be saying they should be sacked, because I think the figures that he'll quote in support of the one he took off the top of his head, are the result of the inspectors grading, branding teachers, and I think that figure will be the result of that branding.

You won't find, I'm fairly certain, that there are thirteen thousand or fifteen thousand teachers who are in the bottom band. There'll be maybe in the bottom three bands in terms of capability. Now we question even that assessment, it's done on a snapshot basis. It's done when teachers are under the greatest possible stress. It's done when they've been exhausted because of the preparation for the Ofsted. And it doesn't reflect, in any way at all the way in which they will teach over a period of time. That can only be done by those who see them over a period of time - the Headteacher or the Head of department. Even if those figures are near to thirteen or fifteen thousand, they're flawed because of the environment in which the teachers are being assessed.

Now if you say, what might the figure be, if you took an early round of inspections, then the number of teachers who are identified to be in the then bottom category, created a figure of something like two and half thousand I think, nationally, if you did it by way of extrapolation. I don't know whether that's an accurate figure or not, because I would still question the method that the assessment has followed, and the circumstances at the time. But it certainly produces a figure out of a teaching population of about four hundred and eighty thousand, that is very small indeed.

If I come back to an earlier question of yours, it's no use saying to the public, you can't persuade parents that if it was two and a half thousand, that that's an acceptable number, because the unacceptability is if your child happens to be in the class of one of those two and a half thousand for a year, the damage that it can do to the development of that child is immense. We can't be complacent about the number. We would want to say that there isn't a teacher whose capability is such that they really are a threat to the development of a child, and the best way of doing that is through the capability procedures that were agreed following the heavy-handed intervention of Stephen Byers.

Interestingly, the local authorities have had to give a report to government on the exercise of those capability procedures. If there are fifteen thousand teachers who ought not to be in schools, there ought to have been fifteen thousand teachers identified by Headteachers and LEA's through the capability procedures. There certainly has not been.

JZ: Can Ofsted fundamentally change? This heavy inspection regime is causing so much stress for teachers. There are no real contexts to Ofsted reports.

DM: I think it can. I think first of all, it has to have a new Chief Inspector, or you have to have a government that when it laid down what it wished him to do, was then going to ensure that he did it. I think Chris has probably strayed too far. I think he personally now would find it very difficult to be a different being, because if he was a different being, people would wonder why, what had happened to him, what road had he been on when he saw this light? I think you need a new Chief Inspector. That's why I was most critical of government when it had the opportunity to bring someone new in, but instead re-engaged Chris Woodhead. I think that's the politics of Downing Street and not the politics of the DfEE.

I think what Ofsted needs to do, it needs to adopt different procedures. The fact that it's not going to give as much notice, will remove some of the burden on teachers and they'll have less time to worry about what's going to happen. But I think you also need to take away from the Ofsted inspection the fear factor of how the report and the findings are going to be used. Unless you do that, you can tinker about with the arrangements, you can tinker about with the procedures, teachers will be fearful of what's going to happen as a result of the visit. The fact that a number of schools will get light touch inspections will be good for them, but will be no good for the other schools. The fear will be, that they just concentrate more and more on the schools where they find some weakness. The more they concentrate on those schools in the hostile way they have done in the past, the less opportunity for those schools to improve themselves.

JZ: Is teaching very different today than it was in your time as a classroom practitioner?

DM: Yes. I think the monitoring of what the school does. The monitoring of what the teacher does. The greater demands, the less flexibility, the different relationship with government, with local authorities, and the greater demands coming from a national curriculum never properly thought through and never properly financed. I think they've made dramatic changes to the job.

A Class Act

9. *Butchers, bakers, candlestick makers*

A who's who of non-teaching staff

There are a great number of people to be found within the confines of a school, who are not doing any teaching or management duties at all. They are busily going about their daily tasks, and appear to be serving the wider community, but who are they, what do they do, and should they be there in the first place?

Canteen Staff

Canteen Staff are the people who actually prepare and serve the food in a school canteen. They are solely responsible for the culinary habits of children during the school day, give or take a few million *Kit-Kats* and packets of *Quavers*. Whereas a hundred years ago, they may have been free agents in the field of lunch preparation, today they are bombarded with a steady flow of directives and despatches. There are healthy eating guidelines as to what sort of meals should be created on their shimmering steel surfaces, and acres of paper have been delivered to their offices, extolling a range of desired canteen practice, from how one should wear one's hair when hovering over a deep-fat fryer, to which utensil serves gravy most efficiently. The one meal they are paid to conjure up is intended to be nutritious, filling and inviting to the young palette. In reality their fare is often so abysmal, that it contains a negative nutrition factor, i.e. it is actually bad for you. However, we do not intend to traverse the well-trodden platform of ridiculing school meals. Those who are forced to eat them are far better ambassadors for this particular campaign.

In reality, 'school dinner' can be pleasant or even tasty, and we know of one institution where teachers actually fight children in an attempt to grapple for the last mouth-watering portions of treacle-tart. There is often a considerable element of fresh fruit or vegetables to be found amongst the sausage sandwiches and familiarity is certainly welcomed by the recipients above any clamour for radical menu variety.

The day of a member of the canteen staff is arranged broadly into three crisp segments:

1. Preparing a meal for hundreds of screaming children.
2. Serving it to the same interest-group.

A Class Act

3. Clearing up after they have all finally stampeded out into the playground.

Just getting the amount of portions right would send many a leading chef into a fully-blown souffle tantrum. Try cooking for eight or ten people. Invite some neighbours in, and swell this number to twenty. Within a very short space of time, you will begin to realise that this is not the same as preparing a cheese and pickle bap for one. We are talking massive trays and dishes, with a corresponding amount of stirring muscle power required. As if getting the substances into containers wasn't a big enough trial of anyone's sensibilities, the delicacies must be piping hot and ready on time. There are no second chances, no 'come back in half an hour when we'll have a table ready for you.' Your customer base is living in the age not so much of fast-food, as of rapid edible excursions. In one school, where a reliable survey was carried out, it was established that the eating duration of an average child was 86 seconds, and that included desert, and fighting with one's dining neighbour.
Visit the kitchens of a school, and you will witness a gargantuan process of chopping, grating, mincing and slicing. OK, in some schools the Health and Safety elements are not stuck to by the letter, with plucky cockroaches feasting on old rice crispy cakes, and a floor so soap slippery that any ice-skating pretender could make a more than passable attempt at a triple salko upon its inviting surface. But, cast these one-offs aside, and accept with assurances that most kitchens are run by people possessing such pride, that they not only boast you could eat off their floor, in some instances they insist upon it. One school recently had a week where all of the children did exactly this, lying sprawled over the canteen's spotless floor, and relishing licking up any spare droplets of tomato sauce from the sparkling linoleum.
The serving part of their day is rarely without an incident so complex and seemingly intractable, that a highly trained team of international peace negotiators would have great difficulty in concluding the episode; pushing-in, tripping up, cheeky comments and sulky complaints are part and parcel of the daily routine, but you won't hear canteen staff complaining or getting confrontational. They have a mission to complete, and until their pile of lemon-fresh plates has diminished, and been despatched to the outstretched arms before them, with a piled heap of goodness upon them, they will not shirk from responding to enquiries and meeting demand. The flare-up's are always smoothed out with the aplomb and subtlety of senior diplomats, "Eat this or clear off" being a particularly popular refrain. The children arrive, are served, consume and depart, and thus the lunch hour speeds by in a whirr of ladles, clattering cutlery and expressions of disgust.

A Class Act

As if they have not already done enough in the cause of boosting the health of the nation's younger digestive systems, Canteen Staff are then faced with the prospect of the aftermath. Once, the space is cleared, it is their task, often on hands and knees to recover every smudge of grease, each sausage casing and all discarded chips - consigning them to the inner depths of the mighty bins. If this is completed successfully, then, and only then, may the great floor washing apparatus be wheeled out, and things set in motion to face the next day.

And what of the children who gobble up their delicacies? Do they show any morsel of gratitude or fondness? In some cases, a most definite yes, but in others, the only sweet-nothing a member of the canteen crew will ever hear is the phrase 'Fish fingers,' with a rare 'please' occasionally tacked on for good measure. To the children, the food may as well be served by faceless automatons, pre-programmed to deal with requests for 'lots of chips', or, 'I don't like that.'

Working in the canteen is more than a job of work; It is an art form, a skill, an act of finesse that no mere teacher, however long they trained, for could have a half decent go at. It is a job fraught with tension and pain, and the plight of these (almost overwhelmingly) women has been understated for decades. Let us stand up and be counted as we sing a collective mantra to the generations of people who have slaved over steaming cauldrons - "Someone's baking my lord, kumbaya."

Of course in the modern age, we have witnessed the troubling advent of the packed-lunch, complete with themed carrying case, and soft drinks attachment. It is nothing short of a miracle that no canteen worker has ever been known to down her saucepans in Luddite fervour, as yet another child turns their nose up at her offerings by delving into the innards of their Jurassic Park lunchbox. As another dollop of mashed potato is dispatched with love, a new face arrives in the arena, bright with the promise of their new status as a pack-lunch child. If syrupy tears of humiliation slide down the cheeks of those at the counter, they are always hidden from us. Canteen Staff will not give in to the advancement of technology, nor will they be outwitted by parent power. They have been in the trade for so long, that even when they finally hang up their wooden spoons and make that last journey to the great serving-hatch in the sky, they cling to the notion that their food was good enough for anyone.

Dinner Ladies

Dinner Ladies are the people who patrol the playground and canteen at lunchtime, and we must stress that this term is not gender specific, and thus includes any men

A Class Act

on the case, and there have been quite a few sightings. The words *Dinner Man* have been uttered, but sound so hollow, that they are rendered meaningless. So even if you see a hard looking geezer replete with tattoos, wandering around in an ex-army jacket, yelling commands at a bunch of screaming five year-olds, to all intents and purposes he is still a Dinner Lady. Having got this linguistic conundrum off our chests, we may proceed.

In various schools, Dinner Ladies are known by different names and acronyms. In some they are called S.M.S.A's (School Meals Supervisory Assistants), whilst in others they are simply L.R.P's (Lunchtime Riot Police). Whatever title they work under, the basic job is still the same. They must: prevent any fighting and bullying in the playground, shout at as many kids as possible, and get everyone in and out of the canteen in record time. They have big hearts and often very big gloves to match, so biting can the savage winter winds be in this country. They would be instantly at home in any barrack room in the world, and would have already received a commendation for bravery if they worked in H.M prisons service.

To work during the school lunch hour you must have: a) Eaten already, even if it was only a light snack. b) An in-built lie detector, and a good memory for faces. c) Incredibly sinewy and powerful vocal chords. If you possess all three qualities, apply for a post immediately.

A school in the middle of the day is a strange and rather mysterious place. Firstly, the teachers who are usually very visible and vocal at all other times, are darting smudges of figures, gliding as nimbly as possible, and in quick succession into the safe environs of the staffroom. Teachers are usually quite adamant that during lunchtime they are not on duty, and must, therefore, be left completely alone. If a child does approach a teacher in this most holy of non-contact times, they are normally pointed in the direction of a Dinner Lady.

Dinner Ladies are experts in crowd management, and can easily double up as line-dancing tutors or synchronised swimming coaches. They shout, and point and usher their charges into a series of unending lines, which inch in the direction of the canteen's beckoning smells. They are armed with whistles and occassionally loud-hailers. Indeed, the use of a thousand watt P.A system hasn't been unknown. In some areas walkie-talkies are de rigeur, whilst in others laptops and mobile phones provide a constant flow of e-mails.

One of the chief pursuits of a Dinner Lady is sensing tension and easing it, before it gets out of hand. Which means that no pair of eyes can rest on one location for too long. A Dinner Lady walks many miles in a week, often held down by burdensome weights in the form of little characters clinging onto her arms. It is rare

A Class Act

to find a Dinner Lady worth her salt who doesn't know every inch of the turf.

Dinner Ladies make extensive use of repeated phrases, such as 'No running', 'Hurry up!' and 'Don't you be so rude, or I'll tell your teacher.' The more astute record these phrases onto small dictaphones and simply play the relevant messages when confronted by a situation, whilst mouthing the words to give the appearance of a live performance. They are disobeyed so frequently, that it is a mystery why so many retain their outward tolerance towards school children. However, some children are very fond of one or more Dinner Ladies, and sometimes call a particular Dinner Lady their 'best friend'.

Dinner Ladies can, and at times, must be ruthless and cunning. But their shared goal is always an exercise in maximising order, so that when the children are handed back to the teachers, they have enjoyed a pleasant and refreshing break from classroom study, and are not crying their eyes out because someone has said they are a 'peanut.'

Caretakers

Not all caretakers are called Jim, drive a Ford Escort and collect old pieces of wood. Mind you, not all caretakers are called caretakers anymore. Some are site supervisors, and one or two are deemed fit to be called premises managers. They all have one thing in common, in that they are the only person for miles who knows how the school boiler works. They are familiar with every nook and cranny on a school site, and it is not uncommon to see a caretaker emerging from a hole you never knew was there, or disappearing behind a door you had never noticed. They clamber through dimly-lit passages and tunnels, ferretting about with pliers and pieces of cable, and if you didn't check on their whereabouts occasionally, they could be gone for days on end. In fact, they *are* sometimes gone for days on end, only to be recalled when a shelf needs fixing, or a peeling door demands a lick of cheap D.I.Y warehouse paint.

One of the many perks of being a caretaker is that on-site accommodation is sometimes provided - be it a flat, a house or a corner of the science room. This ensures that journey time to work is minimal, although one or two do still remarkably blame traffic for their late appearance at the start of the day. Their homestead is strictly out of bounds for the children and often for the teachers as well - unless one member of the teaching staff becomes particularly friendly or shares a passion for repairing wire fences.

Caretakers perform many tasks as part of their multi-layered job-descriptions.

A Class Act

They service and maintain the heating and plumbing systems of the school, they are in charge of school security, and they carry large green storage units around, which are never seen again. They often smoke (roll-up's or *B and H's*) and are often married to a woman who has absolutely nothing whatsoever to do with the school, and rightly so. Listening to your partner talking about the workings of latrines in the boys' toilets is one thing, getting hands-on experience is quite something else.

Caretakers will generally have a go at anything, but it might take them some time to get round to you, so busy are they trying to get round to other people. They will turn their hand to electrics, plumbing, building and decorating, but you know that when they scratch their head and tut in a very disdainful way, then they are drawing the line at some outlandish request to turn your classroom into a medieval street scene. They all possess tool kits smeared in multicoluored classroom-friendly paint shades, box-trays brimming with patch pins, screws and nails, and a variety of spirit levels, measuring implements and industrial marker pens. Manuals are frowned upon - being for mere pretenders, and advice is never welcome except when imparted from their own lips. It is critical for a teacher to become 'matey' with the caretaker, even if this does mean reading up on football trivia from the seventies, or becoming intimately aquainted with the *Collins DIY manual*.

It is impossible to know when one will require the assistance of a caretaker, and bad relations are definitely not a passport to attaining a set of new storage dividers. Enquiries must be made about immediate family and from time to time more distant relatives who sometimes creep up in polite conversation. Thanks, when it is uttered, must be done so graciously and sincerely, for a smile that dances on the face of a school caretaker is worth its weight in shelving units.

A good Headteacher will also get a caretaker on side, praising and nurturing him, until he is putty in her hands. In that and only that way, can a school ever be maintained. A scorned or insulted caretaker means freezing classrooms in the winter, faulty electrical systems, high fuel bills that eat into the school budget, and banishment of staff from the premises at the slightest whim. The odd trip to the pub for a couple of pints or a small supply of shorts does nobody any harm, least of all the Headteacher. By ensuring a loosening of the caretaker's tongue and residual defences, the Headteacher can secure a vast array of promises, which she can record by way of secreting a tape-recorder about her personage, and playing them to the re-sobered individual, when she requires these tasks to be carried out.

It is clear also, that a caretaker should keep a regular check on the school's service finaces, for some schools are wasting hundreds if not thousands of pounds a year by misuse of appliances. For example, a school that leaves their heating on

A Class Act

during the summer holiday, will be none too pleased when the red reminder note floats gracefully onto their accounting desk. The responsible caretaker will be in touch with the gas and electricity boards at regular intervals, and by not making long phonecalls to relatives abroad, may save the school a small fortune.

Caretakers all tend to have an interessting pastime on the go, ranging from the home brewing of beer, to the collection of pre-1920 Bolivian postage stamps. Whatever it may be, they are able to talk about it with flair and confidence, and it is always advised for you to take an interest in their verbal meanderings, for an appropriate comment will most certainly prioritise you in the pecking order for classroom redecoration.

The caretaker's profile amongst the children in a school is very varied. Some are seen so rarely, that they are reported as intruders, whilst some are such familiar figures that they have an input into assemblies, lessons and school outings.

School Secretaries/Administrators

If you work in a school and you fall foul of the school secretary, you are in deep waters, without so much as a plastic hole-punched wallet to bail you out. You need their goodwill badly, and anything other than a solid bond is worthless. Requests for stationary will be turned down, vital book orders will go missing and post will be misdirected to the chippy at the end of the street. Befriend her, smile at her, for goodness sake get on your hands and knees and declare that the sun shines out of the gaps in her word processor, but above all *listen* to her. If the school secretary is just about to commence a lengthy monologue about her husband's bad habits, and your class is about to re-enter your classroom, get someone to cover for you if you possibly can, for a kind ear will earn you that extra ream of photocopying paper or the spare Pritt-stick.

The secretary's office is the scene of a thousand dramas, from screaming children robbed of a favourite stone, to bawling mothers fighting for their child's admission. A family-sized box of tissues will adorn the desk of any school secretary, and she will find her supplies need to be replenished on a regular basis. It seems that the whole of humanity passes through these portals at one time or another, and she needs a range of accents and attitudes to get through even the most straightforward of days.

The school office represents the gateway to the Headteacher's inner chamber, as the secretary possesses the Head's schedule and often controls access to her. A school secretary can display tact and the protective instinct on a scale that would

A Class Act

make many a ministerial press aide blush. Her chamber is the centre of clunking photocopiers, ringing phones, and it is the place where more biscuits are consumed than in the tasting department at Mcvitie's. She is the eyes and ears of the whole school community, and if she doesn't pick up on something, it is usually not worth knowing. Children recount remarkable tales about their classmates, whilst parents share such juicy local gossip snippets, that sometimes the door must be pushed to, and a conversation held in hushed whispers. The local press would do well to add school secretaries to their contact list, for she is likely to hear of any misdoings amongst the local populace well before any hack has even pulled open their curtains to reveal the texture of the forthcoming day.

Secretaries possess documents and files which cover every aspect of school life, and if a tasty bite of the information sandwich is required, then time must be spent in good-natured banter with her, praising her clothes, laughing at her anecdotes, and never commenting on the ever growing mounds of paperwork which sometimes eclipse her face. She can pretty much say what she likes, because at the end of the day, you need her more than she needs you. Teachers are ten-a-penny, but she has the golden aura of uniqueness, celebrated by her electric desktop stapler and ability to gain entry to the school safe. Reports for typing must be neatly presented, orders must be correctly numbered, and requests for money must be so superbly researched and validated, that even the greatest accountant in the land would be unable to sniff even the merest hint of impropriety.

School secretaries follow traditions and rituals which have evolved over years, and it is unwise for them to be challenged about any of their systems. If internal borough mail is sent on Thursday, but you wish to bring it forward a day or two, forget about it at once and visit a postbox. Schools run on strict timetables and to unwielding rules and orders, and the secretary is no different. She will choose a certain day as accounting day, and no matter when it is, even if it is nowhere near the end of a financial year, she will not bend to any advances to change it. And when photocopy paper runs out and the staff are eating the staffroom chairs in frustration at the lack of worksheet-producing capability, the secretary will not visit Office World to stock up and avert a crisis. She will inform teachers that they have overused the supply, and will simply have to wait until the next batch arrives from the educational catalogue, in a matter of weeks.

It is worth noting where a secretary leaves her keys, for when she eventually leaves the building at night, her office is a treasure trove of stationary, and tippex containers. There is no feeling more exhilarating than stealthily creeping about her domain, sometimes on all fours, in search of an elusive ring-backed folder. If other

A Class Act

teachers happen to be passing and are invited into the raid, the crime scene can resemble a full-scale militarily-planned excursion, with light fingers turning over every surface in sight, prodding and twisting until all draws have been fully explored and all biros liberated. Above all, when performing such a blitz, it is crucial to leave no apparent sign of a break-in, so that any trace of petty larceny is undetectable, and even if it is discovered, you should have established a close enough working relationship with her to stand above suspicion.

Classroom Assistants

As their title indicates, these people work at the coal face along with teachers in an attempt to extract some half-decent work from the children, and to manage the behaviour of some of the more unruly pupils. They may conduct groupwork, work on a one-to-one basis, or in some cases attempt to take over the running of the show, particularly where a newly-qualified teacher is around. Whilst they may sometimes argue publicly with the teacher, or contravene something the teacher has said, more often than not they are a welcome visitor into the class, for they provide some adult company and add another set of vocal chords to the equation.

They are often very popular figures, sometimes greeted by cheers on entry into a class, and the most manipulative of children take endless pleasure in trying to play off the assistant against the classroom teacher.

There are now a plethora of courses that train you in the skills of being a classroom assistant, and there is a huge volume of talented people out there who are working for a pittance, in order to take the ease off the school budget. As well as working in the class, assistants will perform a wide range of tasks throughout the school, hearing children read in the library, giving extra computer tuition, or taking small groups out to make rock cakes, the constituency of which is often so hard that they are used to break up concrete on the building-site next door.

Welfare Assistants

These people are in charge of all things medical in a school. They dole out inhalers to asthmatic children, check that bones aren't broken and generally add to the childrens' sense of well-being. *Welfares* as they are known, often form the backbone of a school, and in some cases they are pretty much running the place, with the teaching staff consigned to a role as hapless onlookers. Welfares always seem to be able to be in more than one place at once. As they are sorting out one

A Class Act

mini-crisis, they already appear to be working on the next - so flexible is their role, and so committed their attitude. In the age of modern health issues, there is a great discrepancy as to what welfares can and cannot do. For example in some schools, they are not even allowed to apply plasters, which seems to make their role somewhat redundant. And some schools insist upon welfares wearing surgical gloves whilst dealing with cuts, whilst others make no such requirement.

Many welfares are actually very skilled and experienced first-aiders with training and knowledge. Some pretend they know what they are doing, and a tiny minority haven't got a clue, as often the job description does not demand formal first-aid training. Having said all this, in the overwhelming majority of situations, a child just needs a friendly smile and a reassuring word. Welfares often possess the most uproarious laughs known within a ten-mile radius and their cheery banter is an infectious whirlwind, that has given many a future comedian the initial pleasure of hearing someone performing original material. Usually having their own children, and often grandchildren, they are first-class experts in looking after youngsters in a caring and supportive way - skills that cannot be learnt from any courses or self-help books.

Welfares are often the chief instigators of any social outings and all practical jokes within a school. They are the ones who ensure the hose is in the right place when a teacher needs to be sprayed, and they provide the party poppers when there is something to be celebrated. They can be relied on to organise nights out, get a lottery syndicate going, or put someone down if they're getting too big for their boots. They speak their minds with a candid freshness that puts many an arrogant orator to shame. They are organisational masterminds, and social chameleons, getting on with anyone who walks in the front door of the school. For some reason, they are often exceptionally gifted darts players, and thus possess a corresponding ability in numeracy, from years of calling at games. There is absolutely no harm in establishing a child-friendly 'arrows' zone within a school, complete with 'soft' dartboards, and foam darts. Just to hear a delighted ten year-old calling 'One hundred and forty!' is reason enough to establish such an enterprise.

Students

Many different types of students find their way onto school grounds, but if their subject is Greek architecture they have perhaps been misdirected. Teaching students are obviously the main core group to be seen, and they spend their time alternating between chasing naughty kids around the corridors and offering multiple incentives

A Class Act

to their class in return for excellent behaviour and subservience when their college tutor is on the prowl. In warm and welcoming schools, student teachers are made to feel a part of the community and are fully integrated into the school's life. In slightly colder climes, they end up covering books in the library and consuming their lunch on the soft play area, because there is *not enough room in the staffroom*.

However, it is not just aspiring teachers who spend time in schools. Those studying the multifaceted aspects of the education process hover around classrooms, making wry observations on teaching styles and completeing research studies on the links between school milk consumption and attainment in algebra. Students of sociology, psychology and social policy have all spent time in schools, filling out data sheets, and generally getting in everyone's way. Nursing students often carry out some observation or a placement in a school, to get an idea of the nation's health and to test out their stethascopes. Students, tend to be on their best behaviour whilst at a school, and those who manage to be assertive without being too eager or pushy tend to fit in quite comfortably.

Contractors/Builders

At times, one or more workmen or women may turn up at a school to complete some task that is outside of the caretaker's remit. They usually drive large vans which are too big to fit into the ready-made parking spaces and thus block off a segment of staff cars, which in turn leads to much whinging and rattiness. They have to put up with hordes of children crowding round them and asking them inane questions like "Why are you wearing a scarf?" or "My dad's a builder do you know him?" They usually sit in huddles together drinking tea and munching on sandwiches, and in their lunch breaks they relax. Unless a job is massive, they are normally only in school for a matter of days, by which time their novelty has worn off and the children are re-focussed on persecuting the teachers.

The Postman/woman

This character is treated somewhat like the messengers of old. If the school has been awarded a prize or is on the receiving end of some good portion of news, they are welcomed with smiles and camaraderie. If however, they arrive bearing an inspection report or some critical document, then they can realistically expect to be chased off the premises.

There are some extremely good-natured members of the postal service who will

A Class Act

don Father Christmas outfits to spread yuletide greetings, or Postman Pat garb to participate in a fancy-dress day, and these antics can send children into euphoric hysteria and a lot of running around.

A Class Act

10. *I don't mean to be a pain but...*

Parent Power and schools

Parents by definition have children, and children by law, are expected in some shape or form to attend school. So, in theory parents must have some direct or indirect contact with their child's school. Many in the teaching profession welcome parental involvement with thermally-insulated, outstretched arms and declarations of "Thank you so much for giving us all of your time voluntarily." Others however, utter the famous catchphrase, "Sod off and stop interfering."

Parents and schools

There was a time when parental involvement in their childrens' school life, was confined to getting them to the front gate on time and nudging them over the threshold. For some parents nowadays that is still the extent of their interaction with the building and the people inside it. It is a place to take their nippers out of the orbit of responsibility, enabling them to get on with a few hours of preciously craved-for normality, free of complaining and the incessant demands for dubiously packaged confectionery. Carefully typed letters that are doled out to them by grubby fingers at the end of the day regarding new spelling tests, homemade cake sales and the school's forthcoming closure are tossed straight into the dustbin without a first glance. Open evenings are there to be shunned and ignored, or, if attendance is deemed absolutely essential, a ten minute face-to-face is endured, whilst mentality selecting the ingredients for that night's dinner.

For a section of these keep a safe distance parents, school exists, but the less that is known about it the better. They don't study exam results, league tables, or the spluttering pronouncements of government inspectors. They will only ever be pro-active if some other child has been repeatedly hitting their dear one with a starter dictionary, or if a teacher is unfairly 'picking on' their offspring. At these times, a full stride and ready mouth is required to right an injustice. Finger pointing and "I wanna word with you" are common opening gambits, followed by expletives, and occasionally some pushing. It is at this point, that the teacher in question either calls the rather chunkily-built maths coordinator or runs for cover. These situations are rarely dealt with in any satisfactory way, and more often than not they end with the angry parents exiting in a cloud of disbelief and indignation. From that moment on, the only thing the teacher will ever gain from this parent is filthy looks of Academy-

A Class Act

Award winning proportions.

For a quite different section of parents, school represents an opportunity - an open door surrounded by glittering pedagogic lights that beckon and sweetly sing, *come inside, get stuck in, make a difference*. For these heavily involved parents, school is a window in their weekly timetable, with a host of activities on offer, ranging from helping out in the class, to haranguing the school secretary on a regular basis.

In a school calendar year, there are dozens of events to become absorbed in, making a diary look replete and important. Some of these people end up spending more time on the school premises than their own children, and quite possibly a large segment of the teaching staff. Whatever it is that is going on, they are sure to want a piece of the action.

Naturally as with most things there is a middle ground, and this usually makes up the vast bulk of the parental community. They are on nodding terms with their child's teacher, attend big school events where possible, and turn up at parents evening to check on academic and social progress. Although those in this middle ground will be mentioned in passing over the following pages, we will not be primarily focussing on them. This is simply because tales of bitterness and rage make far more interesting reading.

So if you are a parent with a child in school, how do you get involved? This is a question that has faced parents for many centuries, but it has always been clear that a good starting point (and one where it is possible to keep a relatively low profile) is the Parent Teachers association or the P.T.A.

The P.T.A.

This body is sometimes known under different names - **The School Committee**, **The Action Party**, and in more politically right-on boroughs, **The Fusion of Creators and Empowerers**. Whatever name may grace them, they are theoretically a forum for parents and teachers to get together, with the purpose of raising funds for and the profile of the school. In reality these organisations can often be hotbeds of intrigue, cynicism and recrimination. A delicate balance is required, and a Chairperson who can walk the tightrope of diplomacy with the precision of a professional acrobat. Of course, such people are rarities, even within the circus community, and thus P.T.A. meetings can be as rancorous and vitriolic as any pumped-up student meeting, or branch gathering of the local aromatherapy society.

A Class Act

Money is normally at the root of all conflict. How to make it, how to keep it, how to reluctantly spend it. Parents and teachers arrive at these meetings with a slightly different perspective. Parents want what's best for their children; Teachers want what's best for themselves. Thus an innocuous-sounding discussion about how twenty-five pounds should be dished out can turn into a ferocious battle of wits, with the argument hinging on buying more pencils for small hands, or purchasing an electric pencil-sharpener for big ones.

Many hours are spent in the planning of fund-raising activities - the cornerstone of any P.T.A. worth its salt. These come in a remarkable cornucopia of shapes and sizes, from the small-scale jumble stall, through the medium winter fayre, to the grand and overstretching, Byzantine supper quiz. The aim of all such creations is to make as much cash as possible, which can be fed back into the school community, either in drips or in lump sums. Of course, the financial muscle of a P.T.A. is totally dependent on the catchment area encircling the school. In a less affluent area, a yearly sum of a few hundred pounds raised is viewed as a mighty success, whilst in the wealthier parts of town, ten grand and a raffle with the top prize of a cruise for four to Brazil, is seen as being a mediocre return for all that effort.

To get oneself involved in a P.T.A. doesn't involve any lengthy application or initiation procedures, but simply the ability to turn up on time for meetings, and a skill in the manipulation of Sellotape dispensers.

Once these criteria have been fulfilled, you are at the mercy of whoever is in charge, and your duties will be duly dispensed. This can include rigging up a set of speakers for a summer festival, selling tickets to a Nordic musical evening, or chasing other parents around and persuading them to do what you are doing, an activity that is often met with revulsion and fleeing.

P.T.A. meetings can be things of efficiency and speed, or drawn-out orgies of verbosity dominated by droning voices and meaningless resolutions. When there is money to be spent, decisions must be reached, and these are often vastly difficult. Staff are sometimes asked to submit 'bids' for items, and in these conditions, all hell can break loose. Who is to say that a playmat for the nursery is more or less important than a soft hockey set for the top juniors? Why should there be another xylophone in the music room, when there aren't enough thermometers? Surely reading books for all takes precedent over special pencils for left-handers?

One would hope that these meetings were littered by acts of compromise and sense, but in truth the opposite is often the case, with factions battling to the painful end for their all-or-nothing positions. And, as is the case with many committee-like set-ups, those with the most sophisticated oratory skills often get their way, even

A Class Act

though another project may be more deserving.

Parents in class

"I like helping out in class because it gives me a sense of contributing something, of putting a little back into the school, which after all gives so much to my kids. I mean the teachers work so hard, what with all of that planning and marking and the new stuff the government continually throws at them, that I want to just ease their load a tiny little bit. The children respond very positively to my presence in the class and treat me with the respect they show to their teacher. I know the teacher likes having me there, I'm another pair of hands and eyes, another factor in how well a lesson goes. I don't mind them guiding me or even telling me what to do, I'm there for them and the children, and at the end of the day I feel better for it."

"I'm in there to see what that loony lefty is trying to do to my child. If they try and feed their heads with some wishy-washy notions of citizenship or helping each other out, I can get right in there and put the other point, d'ya know what I'm saying? Classrooms aren't safe places anymore, not like when I was young, and you sat there in silence waiting to be spoken to until you dared open your gob. Nah, the modern classroom is full of all this collaborative rubbish, with kids talking to each other about their work. I'll tell you what that is, that's bloody cheating that is. I bet they're allowed to copy each others' answers in tests. It's all become a joke. If that idiot, has a go at teaching maths through some ridiculous topic, like Messopotamian society, I can take my little group aside and tell them that's a load of nonsense, you need money out there in the real world, for food and cars and wine. So don't listen to that Marxist charlatan, just take the money here in my wallet, look at it, dream about it, and give it all back you little animals."

These are just two of the many viewpoints held by those parents who volunteer their services in the classroom. And that's what it is, it's a free-of-charge service, with no rewards other than seeing what's going on in your child's classroom, and perhaps the odd furtive biscuit slipped to you from the bulging tin in the secretary's office, which for once is not wearing its foolproof chastity belt.

Look around any school, and they'll usually be someone crouching down by a desk or sitting with a small group, or listening to someone read. Politicians have talked about them as 'The mum's army' as if this were a new phenomenon. This practice has been going on for years, with no training and in some cases no

A Class Act

encouragement offered to the thousands of people who help prop up the state education system in this country. Many children need to be heard reading much more often than once a week, sometimes for purely reading reasons, and on occasion for the attention. This makes your job even more complex, and thus the appearance of a willing helper who will gladly spend some time listening to children read and talking to them about books, eases your burden considerably and provides the child with a new and potentially very rewarding audience. Some parents come in week after week, and work with the same child or group of children, coaxing and nurturing them along the way, building up a relationship and adding to that child's educational experience. These type of parent-helpers are unsung heroes, and many teachers whisper a silent prayer for their continued diligence.

Unfortunately, not all of those who make their journey into the class are as helpful or as pliable. In one notorious example, a parent not only continually interrupted a teacher in mid-flow, but actually crossed out the teacher's comments in the childrens' workbooks and wrote her own. She tore down several displays and replaced them with newly created collages, and set homework tasks so obscure, that no member of staff could decipher them at all. She banned pencils from the classroom, replacing them with ancient nibbed-pens and bottles of ink, and was heard several times actually admonishing the teacher in disdain. Luckily her interference ended happily, when she was asked to perform the part of a pond in a local community play - a pull that was too strong to be broken.

There are other horror stories of a similar magnitude: The gentleman who thought he was taking the initiative, when on learning that his son's class topic was travel and transport, took the liberty of driving his motor bike through the classroom window, sending shards of glass propelling in every direction, and every child out of the door screaming in fear. Another woman, offered to teach sewing as an extra-curricular activity, and when welcomed by the teacher forgot to inform him that her skills were somewhat threadbare, and eventually ended up weaving several of the children together, a fact which did not go down too well with receiving parents at the close of the day.

As a teacher, when you invite a parent into your class you are clearly taking a gamble. You yearn for the practical and kind helper who will be sympathetic to your lesson plan and will get on with whatever you ask them to do without any fuss. If you do end up with that character who continually questions you about the national curriculum, demands to see your planning file and spends their time nosing about through your shelves instead of spending any time with the children, then it is best

A Class Act

to have a quiet word in their ear, and be shot of them.

Pushy Parents

Pushy parents are always waiting to see the Headteacher, always in a crucial meeting with the class teacher, always demanding more time. If the school has a football club, they want to know when the netball sessions will be starting. When the netball has started, they will be on the case of the basketball franchise. And when the basketball shifts itself into gear, they will be hot on the heels of the lacrosse round-robin competition.

They will talk in general terms about the school, but they will be wanting to gain as much as possible for their own offspring. If they sense the smallest possibility that new funds may be channelled into school, they will immediately want to know where they are going and how it will affect their children. If there is a residential trip, they will have their child's application form completed and returned before the letters have even been sent out. In short, they are a nightmare for their own children and they are things of terror for those in the teaching profession.

If a work plan is posted up on a wall, not only will they have memorised every detail, they will want to know why certain study areas have been excluded from the plan. Were these intended omissions or lack of care in the macro view? These characters at times take an interest in the school that is so overpowering, it actually slips their mind that they are in fact not the Headteacher. They have been spotted ordering the entire outside of the building to be painted, hiring and firing teachers at will, and in one instance opting out of local authority control because they had read in the *Daily Telegraph* that it made good business sense. They are forever on their kids' cases - quizzing them on chemical properties, when all the child wants to do is eat sweets or play Nintendo.

The children of pushy parents often take on some of their parents' traits, and have been known to utter words and phrases that are not consistent with the linguistic development of a child. After all, it surely must be rare to hear a child remonstrating with another child for their 'tardiness' or tutting at the 'pleonasms' of another child. If they are lucky, they follow their own course of development, ignoring a lot of their elders' antics, and evolve into well-rounded and pleasant adults, who in learning the lessons of their own heritage, are not pushy at all with their own children.

Headteachers try and allocate these pushy parents small parcels of time sporadically, to air all of their grievances and present all of their proposals, but these

A Class Act

minutes are not enough to satisfy their wanton craving for involvement. They have been known to collar the head in the car park after a long and trying day, only to drag her back into the building to complain about some irrelevancy. They call up the head at home (although how they get the phone number remains a mystery). They have even resorted to finding out the destination of the Head's summer holiday, turning up in the same resort, resplendent in swimming costume and weighed down by several hundred sheaves of documentation.

Heads and secretaries have dreamed up all sorts of methods for putting them off and eluding them, but they are so sophisticated that new codes have to be continually installed, for fear of security breaches. Heads have dropped hints, sent letters, used e-mail, uttered expletives all in the name of having a life free from parental persecution, but so thick is the skin engulfing some of these infamous practitioners, that the message does not break through the cordon.

Teachers groan when they see the dreaded face of the pushy parent at the classroom door, and immediately reach for the trusted *Compendium of Excuses*, rapidly thumbing through all those already plundered and settling for being called to a conference on the effect of toothpaste on a child's reading age. Hiding is no good, because they will wait for you, sometimes for days, waving a forgotten scrap of paper you sent to them, or a grainy film of a promise you made several years ago. In some areas, pushy parents are the largest group within the parental community, and how teachers survive in these hell-holes is remarkable. In most schools however, there are only a handful, and by a few skillful sleights of hand and some failsafe teamwork, pushy parents can be dealt with quite comfortably.

Parents around the school

Sometimes, parents are seen around the school carrying out a range of duties that they have somehow become involved with. An ex-carpenter might have been grabbed by the Head and asked to fix some wonky shelves, a local journalist may have been press-ganged into helping out with the school brochure, or a tree surgeon might be spotted putting that towering oak tree to rights. Some develop a friendship with the school caretaker and are seen in different locations measuring lengths of string or hammering nails into old pieces of board.

It has been known for a parent, or a small group of parents to be pro-active and organise some event on their own. This is an act which is unlikely to endear them to the stalwarts of the P.T.A, but their actions can be a welcome distraction from the other drab offerings lounging around in coloured chalks on the school noticeboard.

A Class Act

Some parents take it upon themselves to organise something that will bring the whole community together, be it a summer barbecue, a rock 'n' roll party, or in some instances a Parents versus Staff rounders match.

The last category is perhaps one of the most remarkable occasions ever to be witnessed, as what starts out with friendly banter and back-slapping, ends an unhappy hour later amidst accusations and counter-accusations of cheating and biased umpires. What such a display is supposed to do for the morality of the watching children no-one knows, but they are extremely good fun and ludicrously competitive. There is no more strange sight than seeing the confused face of a child whose loyalties are being divided in the most pernicious of ways, by parents ("Cheer for us or I'll knock your block off") and by teachers ("Support us or you'll never score above zero in a maths test again"). The scores are usually equal after normal time, but some element of injury time is usually allowed for, given the excesses of some members of both teams.

The Summer barbecue or social, is an altogether more civilised and humane affair, generally enjoyed in an atmosphere of conviviality and friendship. Teachers can loosen up a mite, and change from the formality of their self-imposed everyday dress code, to don apparel more risque in its flamboyance and more silky to the touch, whilst parents can wipe off their frowns of seriousness and laugh a little bit, enjoying the chance to have a conversation somewhere other than at the classroom door. The food is often remarkably tasty at these affairs, and liberal quantities of beer and wine are consumed. Jokes and stories are told and re-told as an azure sky descends on the party, and the figures traipse off to their respective homes, only to regroup with their own the following day and bitch furiously about the others.

For a group of parents, the lure of working in a warm office proves too hard to resist, and some end up at the school secretary's side, gleefully dissecting the finer points of attendance records, dinner money invoices, or expense sheets relating to paper napkin expenditure. They make cups of tea, take messages around the school, and are often told information about other children which is strictly confidential and legally incriminating. If they perform their tasks superbly, and a few coppers are heard to be rattling around in the school coffers, then they may be offered some 'as and when' work, with a pay cheque to accompany it. They are very valued by a school's administration staff, and sometimes actually take on the post of secretary when the incumbent retires or leaves.

Some teachers are outwardly grateful for parental help. One hears of thank you cards, flowers and in some cases time-share holdings in flats on the Costa-del-sol. Others are less charitable, either mumbling a half-baked grunt at the end of the year,

A Class Act

or avoiding eye-contact wherever possible.

Parents as role models

Some schools are lucky enough to have intriguing individuals as parents - people who have some skill or experience to share with the children. In some cases, it may be a professional footballer, who can visit the school and take a coaching session much to the delight of the children and the suspicion and envy of the P.E. teacher. A parent might be skilled in some practical craft, such as mantelpiece decoration, and may attend school to display their talents whilst imparting some morsels of knowledge.

Some parents are *writers or actors*, and can engage the children for hours with excitement-crammed tales of their creative lives.

Parents with an aptitude for *gardening or landscape design* have helped to turn even the bleakest of terrains, into places bursting with shoots of colour and sparkle.

Interior designers have made the shabbiest of rooms resound with the harmonious restructuring of Feng-shui.

If these people are not tapped into, they will only go and work for money.

It is worth nurturing their talents whenever possible.

It is possible to unearth some tasty nuggets, when digging around the CV's of the parents in one's school. A plasterer with good presentation skills can give a practical demonstration of their art. A lawyer can instigate proceedings against several of the children, and an accountant can expand on the intricacies of a tax return.
  Not all parental visits and talks will be brimming with success, but it is always worth a go. Behind every face, there is a storyteller, a conjurer or a fine pastry chef, and it would be a shame for these talents to be discarded, merely because of an embarrassment to enquire.

A Class Act

Parents and parents

One of the most alarming sightings on a school's grounds is a confrontation between two parents. It is so distressing because it does not correspond with the ethos of the school, sets a bad example to the children and can end with a swift call to the local police station. A major reason for such argy-bargy is parental involvement with children other than their own.

There have been thousands of recorded incidents whereby an adult has told off another child or worse, told off another child's parent. When this happens, some try to be restrained, but others simply can't help themselves. The 'tellers off' are often authoritarian characters, used to disciplining people, perhaps with a background in the civil service or the East German secret police. It is in the very job description of their personality to reprimand and *have words with*, and so if someone steps out of line they must be taught a lesson.

This is not how many others view it, and several slanging matches have erupted over this very issue, "What the hell do you think you're doing talking to my kid in that way?" and "Go and put your own house in order you git," being two possible retorts to such an intervention. These scenes can get out of hand and ugly very quickly and before punches are thrown, it is crucial for a distraction to be provided.

Unfortunately, it is often up to a member of the teaching staff to separate the warring factions, with a gloriously liberal salvo of statements; "We'd prefer it if you didn't get involved in discipline issues", "When the children are here, they are our responsibility" and "Look, can we all go inside and talk about this over a nice cup of tea and a ginger nut." If the teacher is not careful, they may find themselves taking on the role of an adjudicator at a boxing ring, with the only difference being, a points verdict is unacceptable. Years of inter-family feuding have stemmed from miniscule playground incidents where one party was deemed to have overstepped the mark.

In other, healthier circumstances, some parents find that school provides a pool of likely and suitable friends, with common interests, and much solidarity to be shared. These bonds can last for many years, often well beyond their children leaving school. In some instances, friendship groups are formed, with people sharing childcare arrangements, walking to and from the premises together, and helping each other out in a wide variety of ways. These groups can constitute a highly positive force within the school, and can be extremely supportive of the Head and the teachers, particularly when the chips are down and every kind comment is desperately clung to. They sometimes find themselves getting involved

A Class Act

with fund-raising activities, with the P.T.A, or decide to have a go at being school governors.

They take an interest in the school's welfare, know that results are nothing on their own, and think not only of their own child's advancement, but that of the school in general. Where such people exist, they are a delight to deal with, and are embraced by the staff group with enthusiasm and warmth.

However, some of these friendship groups can take a nasty turn, and metamorphose into small cliques, with an exclusivist membership roll, and a none too positive agenda. They gain nicknames such as *The Mafia*, *The Witches* or *Those bent on destroying the school from within*. They have on occasion phoned up the local press with a health and safety titbit about the school, or even tried to get one of the national papers to come and have a poke around and sniff out some misdoing. They openly complain to teams of visiting inspectors that there is no educative work going on in the school, and that the teachers don't treat their children fairly.

They form huddles in the playground, which emit roaring cackles of terrifying laughter, and look with haughty disdain at all who pass them by. They sometimes take a dislike to a particular teacher, and complain to the Head about the poor teaching going on in that classroom. Generally their venom, although unpleasant is harmless, but they must be watched at all times for signs of further recruitment and entryism.

Can a teacher and a parent be mates?

Friendships between parents and teachers do form, but are generally inadvisable due to professional problems, i.e. you may find yourself slagging off their kids to them after you've had too many to drink. But bridges must be built and can add to the rewards in a teacher's life. Having a chat at the end of a school day is fine, as is jointly staffing a stall at an outdoor event. Going out clubbing and then on an all-night bender is probably not.

Conclusion

So parents, as with every other imaginable group of humans, are a very mixed bunch. Some are great to have around, like a warm jumper on a chilly winter's night, and must be cajoled, welcomed and ushered over the school's threshold. Others are as irritating as a large fly in your bedroom at five a.m, and must be metaphorically swatted. It is up to the school and the teachers to suss out who are

A Class Act

the most user-friendly, and to take every step to prioritise their involvement.

Those of a less savoury disposition with a penchant for causing havoc must be dissuaded from becoming involved by whatever means necessary. If this involves paying for extremely expensive full-page adverts in the local newspaper, or the painting of sixty foot slogans on the front of the school building, then so be it.

A Class Act

11. Are you lookin' at me?

The misery of inspection week

'To be inspected.'

The mere phrase conjures up a thousand none too pleasant images:

Being cross-examined by a parent or elder who insists on checking that your behind ear vicinity is as clean and fragrant as a billboard Persil commercial demands.

Fumbling frantically in your trouser pocket on a train journey as the uniformed official approaches with his clicking checkometer - a swathe of guilt surging through your veins, even though you distinctly remember purchasing a valid ticket.

An army dorm being bawled at by a harsh squadron leader, who will allocate duties to anyone with so much as a cornflake crumb on their personals.

Inspection implies a relationship of power. The powerful inspector towers over the powerless inspectee. In relation to schools, the body that is charged with carrying out inpections is known as the Office For Standards in Education, with its inevitable acronym tag - Ofsted. The remit of this organisation is to send a team of inspectors into every school once every four years. This is not always logistically possible, but if it has been a while since an inspection team has graced your premises, you can bet that another one will be on its way soon.

Since it was established in the early nineties by the then Conservative government, the term Ofsted has taken on several meanings. It has become a verb - to Ofsted, to be Ofsteded. A term of abuse - bloody Ofsted, and a threat - you better get your act together, Ofsted will be here soon.

The Letter

Teachers are a funny old bunch. They're so used to being the ones in power, so accustomed to being figures of authority and guidance, that when the deadly word inspection is first whispered in a staffroom, they get the feeling of suddenly being shrink-wrapped in cling-film - so great is the overwhelming claustrophobia that

A Class Act

surrounds the whole process. It makes them want to bark in a falsetto screech, *I'm out of here baby!*

The rumour mill of a school staffroom is forever spitting out whispered scraps and scare stories, and as an inspection looms on the horizon, many teachers are seen to be checking the frontage of every letter winging its way to the Headteacher's desk. And then one lunchtime, someone just breezily mentions, "Oh, our Ofsted date has come through." This seven-word utterance has as much impact as a declaration of war, and rings with the solemnity of a death knell. If the grim reaper himself were to turn up at that moment, he would be providing light relief to the tension-soaked atmosphere.

Feelings of melancholia and fear sweep forcefully around school corridors when that official letter (warning of an impending visit) lands on the school doormat. Staff members frantically thumb through hundreds of job adverts, hoping to make the leap before they have to face the possible threat of being pushed. The mere prospect of being inspected is a repugnant one, although inevitably, there will be one or two smart-arses who will look forward to the process, taking great pleasure in ingratiating themselves with the incoming inspectors.

To open oneself to complete strangers is to make oneself vulnerable. And unlike in car adverts, teachers can't make themselves small or protect their existence with side-impact bars. When a staff group is informed that an inspection team will shortly be 'making a visit' to their school (a misnomer if there ever was one - 'making a visit' is popping round to your aunt's house for tea on Sunday), those teachers know full well, that this experience will be akin to opening your front door on a dark wintery night without enquiring who is there or asking for any form of identity.

Some in the staffroom may have been through an inspection before, and they will either reassure their quaking colleagues or take great pleasure in scaring the living daylights out of them. Whatever the level of experience in the staff room though, one thing is blatantly clear. There is not an option of returning their kind written offer of a visit by replying **Thank you, but no, we're not quite ready for you.** They will be on your doorstep within a matter of weeks, and if the school is not looking up to scratch, then you better get out that thousand-pack of bin bags.

The Build-up

Over the weeks building up to an inspection, schools become radically different places. People who normally saunter along corridors with the utmost nonchalance,

A Class Act

begin to walk at a feverish pace, clasping impossibly large planning files and pages of government directives. Colleagues at other schools who have recently undergone an inspection are consulted at length, and any fragment of information regarding the process is collected, stored and pored over countless times. Members of staff whom you have never even noticed suddenly become close associates.

As the dreadful news sinks in, people look inwards and make a detailed survey of the state of their own classrooms. These will have been exhibiting (in all probability) the same wall displays since the nineteen fifties. Teachers gasp in horror when they recall that decimalisation has been introduced to this country, and tear down their posters of Bjorn Borg winning Wimbledon. Contemporary work must be stuck up immediately, highlighting the excellence of their current childrens' achievements. If no such pieces exist, then the teacher must fabricate them, adding the appropriate spelling errors or scribbles to make the facade seem real. If a child insists that they possess no recollection of creating that watercolour based on the style of Rembrandt carrying their name in clear bold lettering, they must be silenced at once, and informed that they did do it, even if a small amount of hypnosis is required. If they continue to deny all knowledge of the masterpiece, then small rewards may be offered to buy their collusion.

Classrooms that are usually as dark and unwelcoming as medieval dungeons, become centres of interior design excellence and undergo total facelifts. They return to life as Victorian dining-halls, Egyptian treasure chambers or steam trains. Grotty shelves become ethnically decorated reading corners, and class computers are cranked up for the first time, (when the on button can be located).

And what do teachers say to the children about the imminent arrival of those hawkish infiltrators from Ofsted? This dilemma is the subject of much staffroom discussion. *Should we tell them anything at all? Should we threaten them to be on their best behaviour or else? Should we scare them?*

Most people arrive at some form of compromise, whereby they inform the children that some 'visitors' are coming to see the school, but do not explain the potential horror of the experience. It is crucial, after all, that the children do not pick up on your sense of impending doom and apprehension.

Practice saying the word 'visitors' in front of a mirror, so that it sounds natural and without fear. In this way, you may just as well be announcing that an ice-cream company representative will be visiting the school. Children are generally interested in visitors, so it is best that they have some basic knowledge of what is about to happen, and stated baldly, that is: A group of people in smartish clothes will be residing in the school for a week, looking at every aspect of school life, from

A Class Act

how lessons are conducted to hygiene standards.

As the commencement date approaches, activity within the premises takes on the humdrum buzzing of an all-night grocery store, the only difference being that there's no beeping sound when doors are opened and closed. Any notions of normal working hours are dispensed with, as some slog away around the clock to get everything ready. It is not unusual to spy individuals pacing around school buildings at weekends or during the normally sacred half-terms, as the last pieces of sticky-back plastic are applied and the finishing staples fired in.

Documentation is examined over and over again, and if evidence is not to be found, it is created and backdated to dovetail magnificently with that already in circulation. The cleaners get in on the act, with extra polishing and sweeping sessions, the washing of windows and the cleaning of chair legs.

At a certain point, most people realise they have done all that they possibly can, and they stop, sit back and await their day of judgement. A few individuals get so intricately bound up in the whole process that they are still arranging their desk tidies when the inspectors arrive.

The Regi

Before the real thing kicks off, the staff will have had a chance to meet the head of the inspection team who is known as the Registered Inspector or Regi. He or she will have visited the school to explain to the teachers what form the week will take, and to listen to the praise and grievances of the parental community. The teachers meeting with the Regi is usually held in total silence, as everyone hangs onto each syllable that is uttered, as if their words hold the key to surviving the imminent inspection.

The parents are also granted an audience with the Regi, and this session can be an altogether rowdier affair, and has been known to become a slanging match between those critical of the school, and those wishing to defend it. The Regi is expected to officiate impartially in these sometimes barnstorming rows, leaving the building with a balanced view of the school. In an apathetic area, a small and cynical pressure group may appear to represent the parents' dominant voice, and thus a bit of canvassing by the teachers to ensure attendance of some positive parents is always recommended. This can take the form of a quiet word in a friendly ear, but mailshots and modern door-to-door campaign techniques are not to be ruled out.

A Class Act

Let battle commence

You have dreaded it for weeks. You have built up hundreds of painful scenarios in your mind, of humiliation, insults and ultimately dismissal from your job, and then suddenly it is the night before, and you get that 'Sunday night feeling', but with a multiplication factor of infinity.

Arising the next morning, you leave your abode clutching a wallet of lessons that have been so well prepared, the Dean of a University town-planning department would be proud to call them his or her own. Nothing has been left to chance. If a frozen chicken is required for one of your classes, you will have made that trip to Iceland to purchase the necessaries. If your topic plans stipulates pond-dipping, then you will have sunk a small one inside your classroom.

To be honest, you have never been so well prepared for a day's teaching. Of course, in your student days, on teaching practice, you had everything ready and prepared, but the thought of facing an Ofsted inspector pushes you that little bit further. You do not want to feel complacent or arrogant. But you also don't want to be burdened by nerves and terror. So, you opt for a happy medium, whereby you will be on your toes without shoowing fear, and capable without being aggressive.

There are no second bites at the cherry of curriculum delivery, no "I'm awfully sorry but I left them in the bathroom", no "I had a really late night last night and fell asleep on the sofa in front of the *learning zone*." You have been over every lesson both in waking and sleeping hours and you have learnt your introductions so completely, that an evening recital of your lesson introduction on photosynthesis, accompanied by classical music would be a performance well worth attending.

As you walk over the school's threshold on that first morning of inspection week, there is an air of hushed expectancy around the place. You don't quite recognise your surroundings. Something has changed. Where are you?

For a start, people are wearing smarter clothes, and shoulder pads rub shoulder pads with suits, and for once perfume odours eclipse the nasal twang of cleaning fluids. People, who until now, you had accepted were hideously ugly, have transformed into very presentable humans. The pace of things has upped once more, as colleagues give the impression of getting things done, a situation which makes you feel uneasy.

There are strangers in the building - who have been in attendance since the crack of dawn, opening up the school for the caretaker and collecting the day's milk supply. These of course are the members of the inspection team, and it is critical to study their features for any signs of weakness. If they return your stare with icy

A Class Act

menace, be warned, for they might already be on your case.

These characters have all been through their own version of hell to get here, undergoing a training process that involves whole weekends cooped up in hotels, rushing around completing assignments and conducting role-plays on how to be officious. They stand there, chatting informally to staff, as if this is to be just like any day in the school calendar, flicking through records, and looking with a knowing gaze at all who walk past them. They bleat out a slightly forced *hello*, and offer a handshake as you enter their space, but they quickly withdraw their arm in an initial game of cat and mouse before you can grasp it.

It has been recounted, that in a number of schools as the team of inspectors walks in, an individual teacher or even a group of teachers walk straight past them and out of the gates, never to return.

You hurry to your classroom, and shut the door behind you, knowing that only a few feet away sits a clipboard with an inspector attached to it, who may decide the date of your retirement party. You know, and this has been repeated a thousand times, that the inspectors are at liberty to enter your classroom at any time they wish. They can stay for as long or as little as they please, and they are not required to give you any immediate feedback. They can talk to any of your children, look at whatever work they so desire, and rummage around in your planning files.

Teaching for the week becomes a sort of 'showcase lesson presentation' experience, which is as near to a game show format as it gets, but without the fruity voice-overs and commercial breaks. It is a time of performance, of cheery smiles in the face of crushing adversity, and of convincing the invaders that you are good enough to stay put, at least for the time being.

The staffroom is in an altogether different dimension. Out are the stained coffee cups, and piles of unwanted documentation. In are crisp looking individualised portfolio files, and minutes from the last staff meeting, typed in a mature and sophisticated font. For once, people listen to the Headteacher when an announcement is made, and even the most trivial of communiques are greeted with interest verging on the fanatical.

And then, suddenly, in that twilight zone of a school morning, between the cosiness and security of the staffroom and the daily clashes of the classroom, it is time for the bell to be rung (on time for once), and following a few back slaps and mutual words of encouragement, you are out there, walking the long and lonely gang plank to your classroom. Everyone is looking over their shoulders to see who the shadows are following, and if you are lucky you might escape the first round.

A Class Act

Enter at your peril

An inspection week is one of the most remarkable experiences known to humanity and passes in a haze of jokes, tears, new-found smokers, sordid tales, fear, elation, despair and for those who find it a relaxing pastime, sewing. The inspectors do appear at the most unwelcome of moments. A child has crawled under a desk and is refusing to re-emerge. A group is building a four-storey tower block with coloured cubes instead of working out addition sums with them. A fight is breaking out on the topic table as two children vie for the chance to read a book on canals.

And an inspector breezes inside right in the middle of it all, indifferently nodding in your general direction, perching in a corner to complete their official monitoring form. You scramble around the class, giving off an air of being in command, whilst your mind second-guesses the notes being entered into the inspector's ledger:

This is the most disgraceful attempt at classroom management I have ever witnessed. The children were literally running riot, and if there had been any placards present and a loudhailer, I would have convinced myself that I was in Trafalgar Square on a rally day. Whilst this does stir fond memories of my own student days and the sit-ins we engineered, it is not an appropriate sub-text for the modern classroom.

This teacher is an imposter seconded from an imbeciles' retreat. The lesson introduction was so long and confused, that several of the children actually climbed into their own storage trays to sleep.

The children in this class have no sense of collective purpose. It is as if they are following their own individual lesson plans. Whilst some played computer games, and others held a small fashion show, two children were organising an extended session of crazy-golf next to the science cupboard. Whilst the course they had established showed great initiative in the field of Design and Technology, it had nothing to do with the lesson's objective, which was learning about the eating habits of the Victorians.

The teacher did make an earnest attempt to show the children how to construct a basic electrical circuit, but when they tired of his endeavours they locked him in the paper store, and carried on with swapping football cards.

A Class Act

In all my days I have never seen a teacher pour Shreddies over a child.

Of course, in reality, what is written is never as condemnatory as you fear, and some quite positive points are made. It's just that you often have to wait so long to hear them. It is in your feedback session towards the end of the week that you are told of your progress, a meeting which can bring on sobs of relief or disappointment in even the most seasoned of campaigners.

Whilst an inspector is in your classroom he or she will always seem to organically drift towards the children you specifically want them to avoid. Barring any attempt to hide a child from view (although it has been tried), there is no way you can stop the inspector approaching the child whose ways fill you with dread. You wince as the inspector kneels down and asks them what is expected of them in the poetry lesson and they shrug their shoulders and start talking about their collection of plastic soldiers. However much you intervene and explain that little Dave has 'problems' the inspector will shoot a look at you that says, *This child is unaware of what they should be doing and is not on task. You are a miserable failure.*

For the whole week, you live in a state of constant terror, knowing that someone is lurking round a darkened corner, waiting for the chance to enter your classroom or bombard you with some complex questions that you don't understand. If they are rooting around for the answer to some obscure parable, they will badger you until you are forced to blurt out an answer - a response which may return to haunt you in written form.

Although the teachers outnumber the inspectors they seem to overrun the place, appearing in several locations at once, and springing out from behind bushes when you are reaching the pinnacle of a threat to a child who you insist must behave in P.E. this afternoon, because you know you are to be watched.

The adrenalin flows at top speed all week, as the exhausted staff plough through their lessons, setting up their classrooms for the next ones, and dreading the following day. As the week draws to a close, it suddenly becomes apparent that the inspectors are leaving the premises, and will hopefully not be returning again, at least not for a four year period.

This feels like getting rid of a nasty rash, and you can run around the corridors once again, and scream obscenities at the tray of percussion instruments. Following the tension and nerves of the week, it is difficult to act *normally* once again. You find yourself holding conversations with other staff members at reasonable decibel levels, instead of the previous hushed whispers. You can berate children once more

A Class Act

in full flow without gritting your teeth and trying to sound so *reasonable* all the time. And perhaps, best of all, you may lie down on a sofa in the staffroom and proclaim to anyone in the vicinity that you have no idea what the school development plan actually says.

It is a time of high emotion and it all ends in a flurry of utter exhaustion, much celebrating, but fear concerning the contents of the inspection team's report.

The informal report

And they do not waste time turning their findings into snappy copy. We are not talking experimental poetry, love sonnets or even Mills and Boon, but instead numbered formulaic paragraphs that are less interesting to read than a cinema ticket. They have a rigid set of criteria with which to measure each school, and in a matter of days the Regi is presenting this document to the Headteacher and the school management team, and the terrible truth is there in black and white for all to see. Sitting down with the Regi and thumbing through the report can be a very strange experience. Here you are, in the same room, with a person who has potentially said some very nasty things about you.

Naturally, some schools get shining reports that laud their high educational standards, their Flemish club and archery lessons, and the fact that they have only English-speaking middle-class children on the premises, and therefore no possibility of any destabilising influences.

At the other end of the spectrum, whilst verbally sympathising with a school's extraordinary levels of children with special needs and those who do not speak English as their home language, reports can set about savaging the school's exam results and poor attendance. In short, they drop the same framework on a tiny country school with open fields to roam in and a nature table the size of the Titanic, and on an inner-city school with a graffitied playground, and weeds jutting out through a menacing stretch of battered concrete slabs.

At this informal stage the teachers and school governors all get the opportunity to read the draft findings, and put across their own perspectives. The Regi will listen to any observations or even criticisms concerning the informal report, but will rarely change the 'substantive' thrust of the report. The Regi will bandy about terms like 'corporate viewpoint' and 'collective decision-making' to ensure that everyone knows the report has been written by his whole team. With a whole collection of inspectors to make contributions, most would assume that the report must be a pretty valid and truthful document.

A Class Act

This is of course not always the case.

The formal report

And thus when the real thing appears a few weeks later, save from a few tweaks, it is largely unchanged, and by law the summary section or 'main findings' must be passed onto to every parent or carer with a child in the school.

This is duly done, and parents respond in different ways to the document which is handed to them at the end of a school day. Some drop it straight in the bin, others leaf through it but take very little notice, some read the odd section, and a group will learn the damn thing off by heart.

What follows is a period of time when parents ask a lot of questions, and teachers, if necessary, defend themselves and the school by giving a lot of diplomatic answers. There are many classroom doorway conversations to be had, with teachers explaining that the report was 'generally very positive' with 'a few small items that need looking at.'

Some parents *are* disturbed by the findings of a report, and choose to take their kids away to another school which has had a better Ofsted report, whilst others are simply reassured at their choice of educational establishment.

After all the fuss, all the histrionics and all of the school resources that have been used, the inspection is over. Sure, the inspection team might recommend that another smaller bunch come back and check up on you before the next major inspection. Indeed they might say the school has problems. But in the vast majority of cases, schools weather the storm, and get back to the daily task of educating their children. In really abysmal schools, an Ofsted report will recommend that a school is given a period of grace in which to get their act together. If this feat is not achieved to the satisfaction of Ofsted, then the school may be closed down, and reopened at some later date with a local business running it, for example a jewellery store. This will lead to excellent sales of Swiss watches, but not necessarily to improved reading standards.

The fallout

Whilst many inspections come and go without causing any serious damage, an Ofsted report can destroy the soul of a school. This may sound like an overly dramatic statement, but just ask the personnel of those establishments who have been battered by the raging hurricane that can be an inspection week. Some schools

A Class Act

take months to get over a full inspection, only to find that another one is on the horizon.

Where are the statistics that detail how many brilliant teachers leave teaching because of the punishing force of an Ofsted inspection? Where are the figures concerning all those whose usually energetic motivation has been cudgelled and dampened to the point that they function as a sort of automaton? They have never been calculated because no one has the time or money to pursue such questions.

Ofsted reports and Ofsted as an organisation, put bluntly, command little respect, much fear and large helpings of contempt within the teaching profession. Teachers pay short shrift to many of the findings in Ofsted reports and many see the whole process as an insult of colossal proportions. As it stands, those who are being inspected possess extremely limited faith in the system, and a major shake-up is badly needed, if a serious partnership between government and teachers is ever to exist again.

A week-long inspection costs thousands of pounds, and on Ofsted's present track record this in many cases seems to represent a ridiculous waste of resources and money. Naturally, some of the findings are helpful, but after a week of grilling, all a school is presented with is a list of recommendations that are usually already being tackled on a rolling programme.

Of course schools have to be inspected, it is in the interests of everyone, but surely it would be better to scrap the present heavy-handed system and begin afresh, with an approach that would be amenable to both government and teachers.

The model suggested by Tim Brighouse elsewhere in this book (or a very similar model) is possibly one that would be greeted with much support by many in the field. Her Majesty's Chief Inspector of Schools, Christopher Woodhead, has backed the idea of 'light touch' inspections for schools that consistently perform very highly. But we know in reality the vast majority of these would be schools in more advantaged areas where the pressures are far more limited than in the less adavantaged areas where schools will still continue to be subjected to the full might of Ofsted inspections.

Mr. Woodhead talks and writes a lot about Ofsted. Mr. Woodhead talks and writes a lot about education. He is an extremely powerful man, whose stewardship of Ofsted has always attracted much controversy. Some in the profession agree with much of what he is doing and applaud him for speaking out. However, his skilful handling of the media and soundbite snippets, have caused many a teacher to raise their arms in uproar. There have been countless articles written about his style and tactics. There have been protest letters, challenging his pronouncements. There

A Class Act

have been petitions organised by local branches of teaching unions, calling for his resignation.

So, is Christopher Woodhead as bad as many at the coalface and in the unions believe him to be, or is he a vastly misunderstood moderniser, saying the unsayable and dragging the teaching profession into the necessity of the modern age?

We decided to pay him a visit.

A Class Act

12. Interview with Chris Woodhead

Chris Woodhead spent seven years teaching English in Secondary Schools. He moved into LEA work in 1982. He then went to National Curriculum Council as Deputy Chief Executive and was appointed Chief Executive in 1991. In 1993 he was appointed Chief Executive of the School Curriculum and Assessment Authority. He took up his post as Her Majesty's Chief Inspector at Ofsted on 1st September 1994. Ofsted is a non-ministerial government department set up under the Education (Schools) Act 1992. Mr Woodhead is responsible for the inspection of all schools, teacher-training institutions, local education authority services, adult and youth education, and nursery settings in England. In 1997 he was appointed joint vice-chairman of the Standards Task Force, which also advises David Blunkett on education issues. He has written many books and articles on educational issues, and has been involved in much controversy whilst in this post due to his forthright views on teaching standards and competence levels amongst some members of the teaching profession.

A freezing cold day in the centre of London. The sub-zero temperatures beautifully masked our nervousness as our shivering bodies entered the lion's den. Alexandra House is the headquarters of Ofsted (Office for Standards in Education). We had been granted an interview with Christopher Woodhead, Her Majesty's Chief Inspector of Schools. His reputation preceded him, with many in the trade refering to him as 'A teacher's least best friend.' Within two minutes we would be in his office, discussing educational matters. We knew that without being too aggressive, we needed to ask him some seriously searching questions. As we glided up the building in the glass lift, we felt as if we were representing all of those colleagues who hold such strong views about this mercurial figure.

DP: We'd like to begin with a quote from a speech made by Tony Blair at the Labour Party Conference which we'd like you to comment on. In reference to the state education system the Prime Minister said, "Money is not the only problem. There are too few good schools. Too much tolerance of mediocrity. Too little pursuit of excellence." Would you agree with this assessment of education in Britain today?

CW: Yes I would. I think that things have improved, and that they're still improving, but there's still a long way to go. We have some excellent schools, some

A Class Act

outstanding teachers, but I agree with Tony Blair, we don't have enough of them.

JZ: A 1995 Ofsted document entitled 'Teaching Quality: The Primary Debate' concerned negative media comments. It basically said that Ofsted should do all it could to ensure that the successes of the system got more prominent coverage. Do you think in the years following the report that this has been achieved?

CW: It has got better, but I don't think we're there yet. I think that there are some pretty difficult issues here. I don't pretend that we've cracked it; I don't think we ever will crack it, but I'm optimistic. I'm optimistic because when I read local press coverage, post-Ofsted inspection, the majority of schools get a good report. The press does justice - occasionally it does more than justice - the Headteacher's PR is very sophisticated. In terms of national coverage, we of course list in the annual report outstanding schools. I promoted, in conjunction with government, the concept of Beacon schools. I certainly try when I'm interviewed, or write material for the papers, to stress the fact that good schools deserve maximum credit for what they do.

JZ: In terms of the national press, though, at the same conference, delegates talked about the issue of balance. They were concerned that there was too much unmitigated criticism of teachers. In your view, in the national press, is there an unjust harshness you detect towards teachers and the profession in general?

CW: The sad fact is that the national press tends to divide between those papers that are unthinkingly supportive of teachers and those unthinkingly critical of teachers. My own view is that it isn't, or shouldn't be, an 'either or'. The profession ought to acknowledge that there are problems - serious problems - and there are also outstanding strengths. The way forward is to acknowledge the problems, work upon them, don't be defensive about them, face up to the difficulties. I think the more we do in the profession to face up to the weaknesses the greater the esteem we will be held in by the general public and therefore the higher the morale will be within the profession. There's a virtuous circle there.

JZ: Moving on to the quality of teaching - you have been widely quoted as stating that there are as many as 15,000 incompetent teachers who possibly should be removed from schools. Do you stand by that figure?

A Class Act

CW: We do stand by that figure. As I've always made clear the initial figure was an extrapolation - it was the result of a statistical model. But, over the last twelve months we have asked inspectors to grade teachers on a seven point scale and the evidence that's emerging, and I shall be reporting this in the next annual report, is that somewhere around 4% of teachers, around 15,000 are being judged by inspectors as incompetent.

JZ: So, in your annual report you will actually have figures?

CW: We will have figures, that's right.

JZ: And how do you think schools should react to those figures, is there a suggested mechanism by which something should be done?

CW: Yes, there is. I'm not saying that those teachers should be summarily dismissed. I think any teacher, like any other employee in any other organisation, deserves support to improve. But, we have firstly got to acknowledge the problem and make sure the teacher understands the problem, and secondly, offer the teacher support and thirdly, monitor their progress and fourthly, if that progress isn't good enough or swift enough then they've got to have the courage with their governing body to face the fact that that teacher is not teaching the children as he or she should.

JZ: And that 4% of teachers, we're talking there about teachers who are consistently delivering lessons which, according to Ofsted measures, are below standard and unsatisfactory?

CW: Unsatisfactory, yes, and consistently, yes. I mean, let me stress this. That within the breadth of the Ofsted evidence we do not think that the Headteacher should immediately take that evidence as god-given proof that a teacher is incompetent. This is only our perspective in the time taken to complete the inspection, but we are saying, this is what we think, what do you think in the light of your much more substantial knowledge about your staff in the school?

DP: Another general question, which prefaces another I'll perhaps come on to in a moment: would you agree that, fundamentally, schools are social organisations that exist as part of wider communities and reflect those communities?

A Class Act

CW: Yes, but it all depends what you mean by the word reflect. If you mean that the standards in the school are determined by the socio-economic background of the community the school serves, then I would say no. If you say they are influenced by them I would say yes. So there is an important debate to be had about the precise meaning of the word you use.

DP: OK, do you think Ofsted inspections adequately take into account the cultural context that schools are situated within?

CW: Yes, I do. But I'm not complacent about this. I mean I don't think that we've got it absolutely right. I don't think there is a huge scandal here in the sense Peter Mortimore *(Director of The Institute of Education - JZ/DP)* would have us believe, that Ofsted doesn't pay sufficient attention to social deprivation - in fact, I would take the reverse view. That some of our inspectors tend to make too many excuses when inspecting schools which are serving very difficult areas. Saying that, I'm not wanting you to think that I am denying that schools in inner city circumstances don't face appalling social difficulties every day of the teacher's lives. But I do know from our inspections that some of these schools are delivering the potential of their children. In the end do we believe in a primary education where because a child has a free school lunch that that child is necessarily going to find it difficult to read. I don't. It's challenging, of course, but the potential has to be realised.

DP: But currently, is it not the case that Ofsted reports only require a concise factual statement in order to cover the notion of a school's cultural context, and that this would appear at the front end of the report?

CW: Well, we're also giving the Headteacher much more scope to say what they feel are the salient features of their community are. The Headteacher's perspective on the school has been strengthened and I don't think that the information that we now provide is a cursory statistical statement about the school's context. I mean I think that we present to the school as much information as we possible can, in fact as much information as anyone has got about the school results, nature of the community and so on and so forth.

DP: But do you think that information is spread throughout the report, so that its contents are reflected by past results, community features, whatever, or do you feel that the report must be read in the light of one contextualising paragraph?

A Class Act

CW: Well, I'm not sure I would want the reader to be constantly reminded. I don't think I can make a general reply. Every different report written by a different registered inspector will have a slightly different approach to this issue. I simply haven't read enough reports from this point of view. But what I can say is that I don't believe we have a problem of that kind.

JZ: You mentioned Peter Mortimore, who has been quite outspoken in some of his criticisms of Ofsted. In a recent article he referred to the inspection process as a 'punitive regime' and the article was really tackling the issue of demoralisation within the profession. How would you respond to that criticism?

CW: I think it's silly. It depresses me actually, the way words like punitive are bandied about in a cliché-ridden way. Point one: Ofsted does not go into inspections with the express desire of punishing teachers. We go in to hold a mirror up to what's happening in the school and to reflect, as honestly as we can, the strengths and weaknesses of the school. If there are weaknesses we believe they should be brought out into the open, not because we want to punish a teacher but simply because we do not think solutions to problems are ever found until the problems are acknowledged.

In the long run, and we've already touched on this point - the greater the willingness on the part of the profession to acknowledge weaknesses and deal with them and strengthen the education that's being offered to children, the greater the public esteem there will be for teachers, and therefore the higher teacher morale will be. You do not do the teaching profession any good by pretending things are alright when they're not. That is going to lead nowhere.

JZ: Can you accept, though, that in its intensity, the inspection process can lead to schools, even where they're providing a good quality of education, feeling quite flattened at the end of that inspection week and can take a long time to return to some semblance of normality?

CW: Well I have to accept that because so many of teachers say that, and I'm not going to deny it. My responsibility is to try to refine the inspection process so that it is...so that the stresses are kept to a minimum. There will always be stress of course because an inspection is stressful, but if there are things I can do to make it less stressful then I will. But I do think there are two elements here. One, there is

A Class Act

the process of inspection, but, two, there is the culture of the teaching profession. I mean if you talk to people outside teaching, sometimes they find it difficult to understand the way in which some teachers respond to being inspected. I hope that as teachers become more familiar with external inspection, there will be less angst, there will be less stress and less emotional collapse afterwards.

DP: In the last twelve months fourteen registered inspectors have been de-registered...

CW: It's probably more than that, actually.

DP: ...and Ofsted has also ceased dealing with forty inspection contractors, figures that show that significant numbers of inspectors or teams are not up to the job. We recently interviewed Tim Brighouse who suggested that the training of inspectors was cursory and that great discrepancies occur between teams and within teams, and more importantly perhaps, who exactly is Ofsted accountable to?

CW: Ofsted is accountable firstly to Parliament through the Select Committee, and secondly to the Prime Minister because I am the non-ministerial head of a government department and thirdly, to the great British population through the daily scrutiny of the media. I mean if Tim or anybody else is suggesting that we are non-accountable, I would suggest he sits in the chair that I sit in, and I think that Ofsted is more accountable than any public service in the country. I mean that's the first point.

Secondly, with regard to Tim's assertions, I'd be interested to know his evidence. I've just read his submission to the Select Committee and it just seems to be a tissue of assertions without any clear sense of why he's saying what he is saying. With regard to the registered inspectors who either jumped or were de-registered, my response is that we can't win. I mean if we actually say that some of them aren't doing the job some people will say 'I told you so.' I mean we have 12,000 inspectors working for us. I don't know off the top of my head how many are registered, but it's several thousand. Twelve de-registered, I mean it is a small number. Of course, we can't afford to have a rotten apple in the basket, we have to deal with those who aren't any good, and we will. We will face up to the, I think, mischievous accusation that this proves that whole system is unreliable.

A Class Act

JZ: What about the figure of the 40 inspection contractors because that has serious ramifications?

CW: I'm surprised that it's forty actually (*It was* - JZ/DP) I think we ought to check it before you go because your point is about the number. But if it is forty, then on the face of it it seems a lot. We'll put that into context.

JZ: There's been quite a lot of research recently following up on Ofsted inspections - there's work by Professor Carol Fitzgibbon at Durham University, there's the study of GCSE results in seven education authorities, there was Don Foster's study of 16+ exam results - what these studies seem to be suggesting is that Ofsted doesn't provide the impetus for change and therefore isn't necessarily providing value for money.

CW: Yes, well, I mean a number of responses here. The first is that I think it's naive to argue that improvement should necessarily follow an Ofsted inspection. I mean if you're the inspector and I'm the Headteacher you could give me the best inspection in the world but if I don't choose or am unable to use it, well, then your work is not going to result in improvement. So the argument that there's an automatic improvement after an inspection I don't think holds water.

I'm not a statistician and we don't have time to go into the statistical arguments but we think there are quite a lot of questions to be asked about the validity of the studies you quoted. One point - Philip Hunter argues that that majority of secondary schools' results don't improve after an inspection, they go down. Preparing this year's annual report it seems that there's a 50% fluctuation in GCSE results every year, irrespective of whether the Ofsted inspection has taken place or not. So it's quite complicated and I suppose the direct response to you is that I'm not persuaded by the studies that have been dome thus far, but there are serious issues we have to face up to.

JZ: Just to concentrate on this for a moment more, if Ofsted's remit is to improve standards...

CW: Well, it isn't our remit. I mean we have this overall mission statement which is 'improvement through inspection' which actually was coined before I came on the scene. I'm not sure whether I would have nailed our colours to that mast

A Class Act

because as I've just told you it takes two for an individual school to improve. But I think that we have contributed in a number of ways. The fact that schools know they are going to be inspected and a report is going to be written has concentrated minds in a number of schools and, okay, some of them have got their knickers in a twist and have done a lot of things which didn't really need doing but others have actually improved things in a significant and important way before an inspection. So we have helped to inject a new urgency, a new preoccupation with educational standards into the world of state education in England.

Secondly, we have identified 3% of schools - 10-12% serious weaknesses, 3% special measures - where for a good number of years in many places schools have failed generations of pupils. We've ensured that those failing schools begin to tackle their problems and the majority of failing schools are making good progress. A good number have now come out of special measures. The other side of that coin is - and this loops back to a point you made earlier - we have also ensured that good schools are recognised as good schools. I think that that has done a great deal for morale, though it isn't often registered in the debate about Ofsted. And that I think has had an effect on standards and improvements.

And thirdly, the evidence that we have gathered means that I am in a position to advise government in a position of real security and knowledge about what's happening. And in the long run, if the government take on board the advice I give, big if, then I think that will be another way in which Ofsted will have contributed to the improvement of the system.

DP: I'd just like to go back to a point that you made a moment ago. In response to Jonathan's question about the fall in GCSE results - you made the point that improvement needn't necessarily follow an inspection because if an improvement is going to occur in a school there must be some sense of partnership...

CW: Well, the school must react positively to what the inspectors say...

DP: Yes, I agree with that in a way. But is there not a parallel to be drawn here with teaching itself where a teacher can only succeed in their job when there is a willingness to learn on the part of the pupil, and perhaps even more importantly, amongst the pupil's family and the community in which they live. You seem to be saying that if there is no improvement within a school post-inspection, Ofsted can't

A Class Act

be blamed for that, how then can teachers be blamed for failure when there are wider factors influencing the willingness of pupils and communities to co-operate with schools and teachers?

CW: Well, I wouldn't want to say that Ofsted can't be blamed. I would want to say that it is naive automatically to blame Ofsted, which I think is slightly different. I accept that if the inspection report is wrong or presented in an unhelpful way, then Ofsted is responsible, but I don't think you can automatically argue that it is completely and solely Ofsted's fault. Now, I accept that there's an analogy with teaching and in my answer to your earlier question about reflecting the communities that schools serve, the extent to which the background of the pupils determines their success I mean I said that I think there is a degree of influence here and I think if a teacher is working with a child whose parent's hold profoundly anti-education views then I accept absolutely that it's extremely difficult for that teacher. But I don't think it's impossible. I say that I don't think it's impossible for a teacher to educate such a pupil because there are countless teachers out there who are doing that despite the social disadvantages their pupils face.

JZ: In terms of the language and quotes that emanate from Ofsted spokespeople, sometimes the language is quite general, for example, last week you said 'our very tentative feel for the size of the problem is that coasting schools could represent 10-15% of all schools'. Can you see that teachers would be quite wary of such statements when they are wrapped in such vague language, that aren't based on empirical evidence, that are tentative?

CW: Yes, I can. But I think it would have been far worse to pretend to a certainty that I didn't have. Then they could justifiably accuse me of saying things that couldn't actually stand up. But I was asked a question and I could've said that I had no idea at all which would have been dishonest; or to say what I did, which was to make an assessment based on some statistical analysis we've done which suggests the figure I mentioned. We think that the number of coasting schools is of this degree of magnitude, but we're not sure. We're simply being honest, I would say.

DP: The polemical nature of the debate about standards in education and the 'efficiency' of teachers etc. means that the important middle ground is never approached. What do you think the common ground between Ofsted and the teaching profession might be and how can you rise above the simplistic polemic to

A Class Act

get this message across to teachers?

CW: Well, beyond pious platitudes like, 'we're all interested in raising educational standards' it is quite difficult. Though I don't think it's difficult with teachers and I don't think it's difficult with groups of Headteachers. And I say that from - I visit three or four schools a week and probably speak to two or three conferences of Headteachers, often of primary Headteachers, and it's very rare that I end such a school visit or a conference with the feeling that we haven't communicated or established some common ground. What's difficult is dealing with the people who set themselves up as spokesmen and spokeswomen for the profession - I mean, let me just give you an example. Book of the week in the TES, 'Literacy is Not Enough.' *(Gets book and thumbs through it).* Quotes like "The bleak spectre of utilitarianism hangs over our schools like a pall." You may or may not believe this, but I cite this as evidence from the 'other side' as it were as regards the emotive nature of the debate.

There are hundreds of examples in this, I won't go on. But I mean the point is made. The fact that, in inverted commas "the opposition" - let me put it in inverted commas, choose to react to the reading debate in this way is, I think, immensely unhelpful. If you read, for example, the report Ofsted did on reading standards in 15 inner London primary schools you will not see that kind of emotive language used. Or if you read my annual report I don't think you will see polemical language of that kind. So the polemics for me are unhelpful. I do, however, see it as my role to speak clearly and on occasion in the past, HMI and civil servants have wrapped up the message in convoluted syntax, a civil service-ese, that has disguised the real significance of what's being said. So I make no apologies for clear statements. But I don't think we have gone out of our way to be polemical. It is those who are opposed to what Ofsted stands for that are guilty of the polemicism that we ourselves sometimes stand accused of.

DP: I think the impetus for that book is to question the validity of the literacy hour and the national literacy strategy at a time when what it means to be literate is changing with innovations in the breadth of available means of communication. Do you think the literacy hour will...

CW: Well, I think they've set up something of a straw man. I mean they're saying that it's a straitjacket, that it's "utilitarian." Whenever I stand up and talk about the

A Class Act

literacy hour, I say that it is the best practice we believe in from the inspection evidence, and every school should look at it and think about how their current approaches to teaching literacy might be strengthened by using the materials that the government has provided. But the assumption is not, in my view, that the teacher should robotically, slavishly, adhere to every detail of the literacy hour. So I don't think there's an issue here. And I think those people who do not like and I think this underpins it - the Word level work, the phonics work, are setting up the straw man of totalitarian imposition as a way of undermining an approach that doesn't sit comfortably with their approach. I mean Margaret Meek in this book says literacy cannot or should not be taught - she actually says that. Now if she believes that she's not going to be sympathetic to any literacy hour, whatever its contents.

DP: But, although you're asking teachers to reflect on their own practice in the light of the structure put forward by the National Literacy Strategy, do you not think that teachers will feel an autonomous modality at work in the Framework for Teaching - I mean there's lots of oughts and shoulds in there, giving the document a statutory 'feel'. This sort of discourse doesn't readily invoke notions of reflection, partnership or interpretation does it? I don't think the message you've put across actually comes through the text itself.

CW: No, no, maybe it doesn't. I haven't looked at the text recently enough or closely enough to be able honestly to reply to you. And I think the way it's been mediated in some authorities runs counter to some of what I've just said to you. I do have some sympathy with the reaction that you're putting to me here, but the good side for me is that many of the schools I've visited, many of the Heads and teachers I've talked to over the past few months have actually found it a tremendous help. They've said that far from undermining their practice it's actually enhanced their professionalism because they haven't had to think about what they are teaching every lesson. They have been able to concentrate on engaging with the individual children in front of them. Their professionalism comes in mediating the overall teaching strategy. I've got a lot of sympathy with that. I mean it seems to me nonsense that schools across the country have been left to find their own salvation, completely on their own, you know the midnight oil writing the policy documents, one school and another school and they're all much the same.

I mean why not give the schools the evidence from our inspection of what works

A Class Act

and then leave it with the schools to judge, OK the language might be wrong, but the principle, leave it to the school to judge how much they take on board. The principle being of course, intervention in inverse proportion to success. The most successful schools, if they don't want to use the literacy strategy then fine, but if a school is demonstrably failing in teaching its children to read then I'd expect those schools to look very, very hard at the literacy strategy and if they choose to reject it, given their history of failure then I don't think that's a very tenable position.

JZ: Does it bother you personally that in many staff rooms you have become something of a hate figure, a pantomime character?

CW: Well it doesn't bother me personally. I think if I was the sort of person who felt worried or undermined by that sort of antipathy I'd have given it up a long time ago. It worries me though in terms of getting the message across and it worries me too because of what it says about the teaching profession. I mean the need to demonise "the opposition" is an index of insecurity. It should be possible for the profession to enter more responsibly into the debate. But as I say I am optimistic when I talk to teachers. Very rarely do I feel that there is this demonisation that's impossible to get beyond. The problem, I think, is in books like this and often on the pages of the Times Educational Supplement.

JZ: What about the role of the unions in this. I noticed, for instance, that on a recent cover of the NUT magazine, *(The Teacher)* you were caricatured as a cat lapping up cream with Tony Blair stroking you. Do you feel the unions are stirring up trouble?

CW: Well, of course they do. But in a curious way I think that that is right and proper. I mean the job of a teaching union is to represent the best interests of its members and the NUT is interested in getting more pay for teachers so they are bound to attack my pay increase. There seems to me something almost respectable in that because it's an example of a union doing what it should do. What is less easy to defend is academics who should be taking a much more dispassionate view being unable to take that dispassionate view. So I don't like the NUT stance but I can understand it.

JZ: On the point you touched on of the culture in the profession. Do you think there is a closed-mindedness about teachers, a kind of harking back to the 70's, where

A Class Act

teachers are not open to Ofsted, that they haven't fully opened their minds to what you're trying to do?

CW: I think we've still got a way to go in opening minds. But we're in a far healthier state than we were 5 years ago. I'm very optimistic about that. I've just written an article actually, which I don't know where to publish, or whether to publish, but it talks about the culture of deference and dependency amongst the teaching profession which worries me a great deal. I mean deference in the sense that I watched an audience of teachers who had listened to a professor of education a week or two back. Now I thought that his speech was appallingly boring, appallingly theoretical, but the teachers thought it was good. Any when I talked to them afterwards they thought it was good because this man had read all the theory, he really knew everything that academics had to say on that particular topic. Now I think that kind of deference to academia actually undermines professionalism.

Also I think that the LEA advisor too - the argument that immediately after an inspection the school needs support from the local authority - when Tim Brighouse says that no school can maintain the drive to raise standards on its own I think he's wrong. You see I've got much more faith in teachers and Headteachers to understand what needs to be done and I think the more groups or individuals outside school - be they academics or advisors, set themselves up as experts who've got access to a wisdom that teachers don't the more you are going to undermine the professionalism of teachers. My sort of drive is not to tolerate weakness, but to identify and celebrate the success and to build on that success and then to effect the cultural change in that way.

DP: Just to pursue this point still further, my feeling, and I may be wrong, but my feeling is that the 'middle ground', the desire to improve children's learning at key stage 1 and 2 is occupied by the majority of teachers. I don't know whether this is a manufactured thing by the media or a reality, but put it this way, there is as much daylight between academics and teachers as there is between teachers and Ofsted. I'm not convinced that the majority of teachers are that au fait with current academic research or are interested in it. I feel that teachers are going about their business, by and large doing a very good job, but remain voiceless in this debate, do you see what I mean?

A Class Act

CW: I want to give the good teacher the voice. I don't think we should give the voice to those who are not demonstrably doing the job. Those who are, they are the people who know. This is why I advocated the Beacon School concept. Because I think the way forward in raising standards is to make sure that those who are actually doing it are the people that try to impact on the wider community. I've got far more faith in teachers than I have in local authority advisors or academics who have not done it. I mean most of the people who write about literacy in this book *(Literacy is Not Enough)* have never taught children. They haven't got the personal experience of it. They pontificate about it as if they had god-given direct insight into the wisdom of it all.

JZ: Could I just follow up something we talked about earlier - the nature of the reports and the notion of context. We talked about differentiated reports and the fact that maybe some schools won't be inspected as regularly as others. Do you think you would like to see more weighting given not just to free school meals statistics, but also the number of children in school with English as a second language?

CW: Well I think we've got to make a distinction between the use of statistics for school improvement and the use of statistics for accountability. On the latter I think there is a danger of confusing the lay person, the parents, with all sorts of statistical perspectives on the one school: the value added perspective, benchmark perspective, absolute data. When we inspected Tower Hamlets they were trying to convince us that they were the best local authority in the country despite the fact that the standards were right at the bottom of the KS2 tests because if you looked at in a particularly statistical way they were making good progress. Brighouse says the same in Birmingham. The rate of progress he says in Birmingham, is twice the national average. Therefore Birmingham must be twice as good as any other or most local authorities. But he fails to acknowledge of course the fact that if you are improving from a very low base line it is easier to double your performance. So I think there's a danger of obfuscating the issue.

But value-added for the internal management of a school is, I think, absolutely right. And the better use we can make of it the more likely we will be to see standards rise. Though I do think that you can have statistically very sophisticated data rich schools that are also management weak schools, and if they're management weak, then they'll continue to languish in the standards doldrums, whatever the data that we give them.

A Class Act

I'm worried about free school meals. I'm worried about ESL. I'm worried about any proxy indicator of prior attainment because so many Headteachers are writing to me. We've got a bit of a crisis at the moment - one governing body refusing to publish their results because they feel that the use of the free school meals indicator puts them in the wrong category of school. They feel that they're not being compared like with like. They live - it's in Wokingham actually and the local population, they argue, everybody is in work so nobody claims free school meals, but the culture is profoundly anti-educational because most of the people, using their argument, have come from the East End and so the simple use of free school meals doesn't do justice to the complex reality. So what I want to get to, if we have value-added and all this sort of thing is prior attainment - you know the actual test results. The problem with that is, that we're not yet in a position to fully guarantee the validity of the application and marking of those tests.

JZ: Can you force them to publish that report?

CW: We can legally. I mean legally they've got a requirement to publish it. But I mean I don't want to get into the position of having to do that. Really the issue for me goes beyond the school. I think they have a point you see, but Ofsted is linked into the DfEE and QCA agreements about the use of data.

And the agreement is that we use free school meals and ESL as the indicators that determine where a school is benchmarked, but I'm becoming, as I said already, increasingly worried about that. I don't think it's fair. I think the right way to do it is to use test results which show, irrespective of background, what the kids are capable of doing.

JZ: As a last question - if we could move back in time and Ofsted were inspecting your class when you were teaching English, how do you think you would have been described?

CW: I don't think I'd've been described in quite the way the Ted Wragg caricature would have you believe. I think that I probably made more use then of group work and individual work than I would now. I'd do more whole class teaching. Then, as now, I was very, very determined to try to ensure that as many pupils of mine as possible came to appreciate great literature. I suppose that was my primary goal as a secondary English teacher, and I very much continue to believe that that is

A Class Act

desperately important.

I think, too, that whatever my interest in, and enthusiasm for creativity, I was also concerned to ensure that children mastered the mechanics of language that I thought then, and I think now, all creativity depends upon. So I wouldn't like to tell you what grade I'd get, but I think it would be a picture of that kind.

A Class Act

13. *How to terrorise a small village*

Taking children on school trips

All too often we forget how little some children have seen of the world. Whilst a few are dragged around to every gallery, historic sight and nightclub their parents wish to attend, a whole handful of others haven't yet crossed to the other side of the road. Thus schools take it upon themselves to introduce their unsuspecting charges to a diverse range of places and activities that occur outside the walls of the school. It is a practice that has been going on for centuries, but for some teachers the reality of the school outing causes untold discomfort.

Winnie Hunt, a retired schools inspector from Rusholme, has a recurring dream. In it, she is asked to choose between the lesser of two evils. A booming voice commands her to pick one of the following options:

a] to walk down Oxford Street at lunchtime on December 24th wearing nothing but a worried expression on her face.

b] to take responsibility for a class of 30 pupils on a school trip to the Natural History Museum.

For many the choice would be an obvious one. They would forego the shame and embarrassment associated with naked bipedal perambulation and opt for the relative safety of the museum trip. Yet, for Winnie who has had extensive experience of working with school children the solution is fraught with ambiguity. Lay people and politically correct parents will think Winnie mad as a fish. Choose the school trip they intone - it will be fun. Anyone, though, who has worked for any length of time with real, live, misbehaving children will surely empathise with Winnie's procrastination. Her dithering, her reluctance to answer the omnipotent, invisible interrogator is evidence that the school trip, whilst masquerading as an innocent act, has the potential to ruin teachers' careers and turn pupils into gibbering wrecks of moral ineptitude.
    Winnie's story - a case of post-traumatic-stress-dream-disorder - is not an isolated one. Long and weary is the road travelled by the organiser of school trips and even longer and more wearisome is the litany of complaints they are able to reel off at a moment's notice. The following extracts are included by kind permission of

A Class Act

patrons of The Golden Wheatsheaf public house.

There was one boy, particularly bright and unusually mischievous, who convinced the farmer that I had been sneaking out of my room at night to interfere with the livestock - the sheep in particular. I'll never forget that farmer bearing down on me demanding an explanation. What did he mean exactly by interfering, I asked. But semantics was not his strong suit and he thrashed me about the cheeks with his riding crop. This was in the old days, before corporal punishment had been abolished, so the boys saw nothing strange in his savagery. Afterwards, I asked the boy in question why he had spread such malicious gossip about me. He smiled at first and then, coyly, he bleated.

We were on board a replica of Columbus's ship the Santa Maria. This was three years ago now, just two weeks before she sank off the Isle of Wight. They tried to tie it in with our visit, but there was no proof. We talked about it in class. Nobody owned up. That's good enough for me, it should be good enough for the authorities.

Why bother to go on trips at all?

The purpose of the age old tradition of the school visit is beyond question. The aim is to broaden the learning experience of the child by facilitating an interaction with resources too scarce, too valuable or too big to make an appearance in the classroom. It can't come to the children so the children must go to it. There are other fringe benefits associated with this and they include:

* The opportunity for children to mass together in intimidating numbers on public transport and thereby act as a barometer of social opinion towards youth culture (very good for sociologists).

* Scope to feed the fauna of our land by liberally scattering the unwanted contents of packed lunches on pavements, along hedgerows, down staircases, on train tracks etc.

* The opportunity to test the teacher's upper limit threshold for embarrassment by having him/her occupy a bus filled with children for whom he/she is responsible as they all sing (badly) 'Firestarter' by The Prodigy, and attempt to make the driver's hair stand up like Keith Flint's.

A Class Act

* The chance to create long queues of traffic as class 3B crosses the A1000 in fits and starts, thereby creating a green, environmentally friendly corridor of carbon-monoxide-free air.

'Extra Bodies'

Having made the bold decision to take a group of children on a trip, a teacher needs to approach a range of other adults, cajoling and bribing them if necessary to join this proposed outing. And what would school trips be without those 'extra bodies' who accompany classes on day trips to museums, plays and areas of natural beauty like the local shopping centre? We speak of course of the parent helpers, welfare assistants and dinner ladies who accompany groups when they leave the premises. When a group of kids goes anywhere excitedly by foot, on a train or a bus, you can be sure that the line of little heads will be dotted with a few responsible adults, steering them back to the pavement and in the general direction of the chosen destination.

These good folk take it upon themselves to shepherd a small group around wherever it is they are going, accepting responsibility for their group members, and meeting up with the teacher and the rest of the class at a certain pre-arranged time. Some teachers with no sense of justice, but a determination to have a trouble-free day, actually assign the most difficult children to these poor unsuspecting, unpaid helpers, who then spend the best part of a morning or afternoon trudging around with a bundle of mischief. This is thankfully a rarity, as most teachers hand out the easier charges, whilst keeping the troublemakers for their own group. This ensures i) they can keep an eye on them and ii) the rest of the kids in that group have an abysmal time.

Whilst trips have become more and more adventurous and exciting over the passage of time, the largest chunk of the outings pie-chart still clearly indicates that local visits are the most popular choices. For the teachers, at least.

Visits to Places of local interest

What may appear to be the most mundane of trips to an adult - a walk to the newsagents, a stroll past the bowling-green, an inspection of a new lamp-post, may open up a box of adventures to the young and enquiring mind.

The door of exploration is there to be rapped upon, for on the threshold of every

A Class Act

school there exists a plethora of visitable sights, providing opportunities for questionnaires to be completed, data sheets to be filled in, and local people to be harangued. How often have you seen a group of children out and about, keeping tally sheets for the number of cars passing over a certain zebra crossing, or constructing a scatter graph of all those in the area who are sporting lycra-enhanced clothing? There is much to be learnt from the world outside the classroom, and full marks to any teacher who attempts to exploit their surroundings.

Some local places of interest will declare their readiness or possibly delight at a proposed sojourn with them, and may even lay on some special treats. Grocers have provided animal-shaped apple segments for visiting children, tourist offices have proffered information brochures, whilst car mechanics have delivered scraps of old carburettors for the children to chew on whilst they pontificate on the wonders of modern fuel efficiency. Of course there will be some people in a local populace who do not relish a bunch of kids prying into their business, especially if they are illegally trading in small-arms, and thus some premises carry placards proclaiming 'No school groups', or house wooden boards to block out any possible sightings of activity within. Tact and diplomacy are the bed-rock of any request to visit, and the rejoinder 'some of them are totally crazy' to an enquiry concerning the behaviour of your group, will gain you a passport to nowhere.

When visiting a local mainline railway station you will know your trip is going badly, if you see the 14:15 westbound train pulling out of its siding with one of your children at the wheel. Likewise on a visit to a nearby post-office, when a child places themselves on the scales to be weighed, and ends up with a seventeen pound stamp on their shirt collar, it is time to vacate the building.

It is always worth phoning a destination prior to a visit, to ensure that the place is open and will welcome an invasion of children. For example, a journey to the police station without a warning call, may lead to several arrests, and a proportion of your class spending the night in cells, with nothing to occupy them other than colouring in pages of minutes from the latest neighbourhood watch newsletter.

Even on the simplest of outings, there is no harm in spending some time at the planning table, working out which route to take around the local park or which benches to sit on for an outdoor drawing lesson. If you are feeling peckish, a visit to the local chippy can be very worthwhile, for as your children ostensibly observe the start of frying time, you can be stationed round the side of the building cramming as many chips into your insides as your mouth will allow. Some educationalists have even been known to leave a class outside the local watering-hole to complete very detailed observational sketches of local architecture, whilst

A Class Act

they nip inside for a swift half.

Further afield

Some bold teachers are not satisfied merely with stepping outside the safety of their base, but insist on taking great strides to propel the children further afield. In these situations, a rather more detailed type of planning is required.

Getting there

Once a commitment has been made to venturing outside the local neighbourhood, extra provisions must be set in place for transporting one's group to their destination. For long journeys, the luxury of a private coach may be deemed necessary, and these come with a range of in-house services, from a snack vending-machine to an on-site pedicurist. With children sitting in twos, it is generally possible to maintain some form of order, as long as the ash-trays have been previously emptied from the last lot of bingo-attendees. If this is not the case then sooty clothes and ash-splattered floors are the order of the day.

The extended seat at the back, with its untold attractions can cause some difficulties and tends to become the source of some mischief. In order to combat this threat, the strategic placement of one of the harder members of the teaching staff in this sensitive area is always recommended. If the bus has a microphone and a good set of speakers, then teachers can provide excellent guides or act as hosts for extended sessions of karaoke.

If a coach is not required, then public transport is entrusted with the safe carriage of the children. This mode of travelling has two glaring disadvantages:

a) children have to mingle with members of the general public.

b) it is harder to keep your eye on a large number of kids in a crowded train carriage or over two floors of a bus.

In reality the best that can be hoped for is an eventless journey with noise levels restricted to an acceptable minimum. If trouble is brewing, it's critical that you get to the perpetrators before they have the opportunity to strip as many seat covers as they can, and transform the material into limited edition puffa jackets.

A Class Act

Museums

Child-friendly museums with their buttons to push, levers to press and panels to turn, hold enough delights to add an extra hour to any trip, as you search in vain for the last group, who are hiding in the simulated oil-slick in the basement. And yet those without any gadgetry whatsoever wear the unpleasing whiff of a poor maths lesson, and the cry of 'when is it lunch?' resounds from the moment of entry. Therefore, it is best to strike at some form of compromise, whereby there *are* interactive activities, but they are situated in contained spaces.

Some children will have never visited a museum before, whilst some bear the weary countenance of those who have endured an overdose. Whilst obvious to many in the adult community, it is worth pointing out to the children at an early stage in a museum visit, the fundamental differences between a playground and a museum. For some children this is a hard concept to grasp, and they will spend a portion of their time mounting priceless Andalucian horse sculptures, whilst challenging others to 'come and get me.' This sort of behaviour is not looked upon in any tolerable fashion by museum attendants, and any breakages are met with blood-curdling screams that emanate from the restoration department.

'Do not touch' signs and *'Stand well behind the rope'* banners are no deterrent to the investigative visitor, and thus there will be occasions where it is possible to spot a child staring out from behind the bars of a recreated Tudor prison. However harsh the dressing down, for some children the lure of forbidden pastures is so great that they will immediately shoot off to explore the other 'out of bounds' areas. In most museums nowadays there are a series of dark coves, which provide a small slide show or topical film. Whilst these are very welcome distractions, the paucity of seating space and the cramped conditions often lead to huge punch-ups, with members of the public joining in for good measure.

Museums also have some in-built queuing requirements, especially for popular exhibits, and if one group have not been well schooled, then pushing-in is more than likely to occur, which not only causes ill-feeling with general visitors, but can also lead to a showdown with another gang of schoolchildren who are waiting their turns patiently.

If one of your charges is playing rounders with the Magna Carta or is using a manuscript page from an original Brahms composition as a serviette, then dramatic action may be required, and this can take the course of flying rugby tackles, utilisation of a handcuff exhibit, or a harsh public pronouncement, the aim of which is to embarrass the child and force them into submission.

A Class Act

As it is unwise to prowl around a museum in one vast pack, it is advisable to break off into smaller sub-sections, with one adult commandeering between five and eight children. Some adults will trust their group members implicitly and feel safe in the knowledge that at rounding up time, all of them will be present. Others of a less generous persuasion conduct head-counts every twenty seconds..

There comes a time in the course of every museum visit, when the children are granted a chance to enter the museum shop. This can prove to be one of the most trying experiences of one's adult days, as a horde of creatures flock upon every pristine display, so lovingly finalised only moments earlier, in their quest to touch and taste each artefact in sight. Their stampede is a packagers' nightmare, as a litany of gift wrapped items are strewn throughout the store and left forlornly in their wake, as they suddenly realise they only have twenty pence, and a pencil is the limit to which their funds will stretch.

The heroic shop assistants weather this consumerist storm with gritted teeth and hushed calm amongst the flailing arms. They are sometimes specifically given the task of dealing with school groups, as the management try out their mettle and watch with relish through a one-way mirror behind the vase selection. A museum shop is almost unrecognisable following the departure of a school party, and it can take hours to remedy the chaotic shavings, only for a new group to burst through the steel doors and the whole process to kick in once more.

There are people who are employed by museums with the sole responsibility of aiding school groups. These are often former teachers, tired and bedraggled after years in the classroom, and delighted with the opportunity to lose a group when necessary by deftly leaping into the service lift and pressing 'Ground'. In the inner depths of the museum, amongst the half covered statuettes and unframed portraits, they can enjoy a quiet cup of tea with a colleague and return to the fray minutes later wearing a quizzical facial expression.

Art Galleries

These fine institutions provide their own unique educational experience, and outings to art galleries pass off very smoothly so long as thick wax crayon is not applied to any exhibit. Arrangements can be made at many galleries, for a member of staff to talk to the children in depth about several famous paintings, an event which might appear a tad boring to the young ear, but in practice can be enthralling. Observing not only colour, light and texture, but *why is that man wearing purple tights?* can prove a very stimulating way of spending twenty minutes. The sheer

A Class Act

vastness of some paintings dazzles children as elegant mayors and fearful baronesses loom over them, bathed in ancient shades.

If a child takes a particular interest in one picture, they may attempt to dislodge it from its holdings and slip it into their lunch-box. This will cause serious problems, as screeching alarms will be detonated, and in some instances metal grilles will come slamming down, and only by the grace of a deftly executed James Bond roll will anyone be able to exit. If a painting is sneaked out of a gallery, it is better to relieve it from the child and either return it anonymously to the gallery, or seek out one of the less reputable members of the art dealing fraternity.

The comfortable benches provided in certain sections of galleries are perfect for many child-centred games, although sword-fighting with pencils is probably not a wise idea. In some cases these facilities can be only to welcoming and several children may take it upon themselves to curl up and get in a quick nap, only to be woken by a teacher who is ready to start the journey back to school.

Fun days

These are generally seen as trips possessing little or no formal educational content, but allow children the chance to experience something that is pleasurable, or travel to a location away from their their local vicinity. These can include days at the funfair, seaside trips or cycling expeditions. For some the freedom is as bountiful and warm as the first ray of the awakening summer sun, whilst for others it is simply too much. For this latter group, the lack of boundaries is exploited to their own ends as they dismantle climbing equipment in the local park, or drink most of the water in *The Aqua Experience.*

On such days teachers can invariably let their hair down, and if it is cropped they may require extensions to participate fully. It is here that children can gain a small insight into the human mechanisms of their pedagogues, as they witness teachers smiling, eating lunch and even laughing. Away from the environs of formalised structures and directed hours, teachers can relax a little, talk to the children in a slightly warmer tone and wear jeans.

When visiting a coastal resort, it is always a good idea to have checked out the amusements on the peer, for if one does not exercise due caution, it is possible for one child to plough through the entire class spending money for the day on slot machines. In addition, rides and attractions may prove to be unsuitable for the age-group you are taking, and unless a firm hand is shown, peer-group pressure may cause even the most timid of souls to embark on riding the unfathomably terrifying

A Class Act

rollercoasters, whilst you are only able to look on helplessly and pray.

Residential Trips

Normally, though not exclusively taking place towards the upper end of primary school and throughout the secondary years, the phenomenon of the residential trip is one anticipated with equal measures of fear and euphoria. Fear, because the prospect of spending a week away from the safety of your own sofa in the company of children whose overriding objective is to impress their mates in an out-of-school situation is one second only to naked skydiving for sheer exhilarating terror. Euphoria, because:

a) you're going to be out of your classroom all week, and,

b) you are in moments of naivety, tempted to dream of surviving the trip and wearing the invisible badge of courage with pride.

So many factors feed into the residential trip experience that it's worth looking at each one of them in turn.

Worried Parents

For many parents this will be the first time they've let go of their offspring. The first day of school was one watershed, leaving the child at the gates and walking home to an empty house, the silence deepening every minute until normality returned at four o'clock. Similarly, this waving goodbye parents do before residential trips, this ritual leave-taking, is a big moment in the whole panoply of parenthood. You, the teacher, as the 'responsible adult', will be brow-beaten by an orderly queue of concerned mums and dads, aunties and uncles, who will give you a list of do's and don'ts, wills and wont's, have's and haven'ts, ailments-past, ailments-present, and ailments-yet-to-come.

You will be asked to remember that Jack sometimes wakes up and needs a little drink of water; that Aisha might sleep walk so could you ensure she's not near the staircases; that Connie needs her foam toucan in order to get to sleep. As the coach pulls away, the huddled adults who are waving frantically are, unbeknownst to them, rebuked by their young charges for even considering such action necessary.

You hear the complaints of the children, their hissing and cursing and heavy

A Class Act

sighs, their barked commands, "Go away!", their holy exclamations, "Oh God, mother!" And as the coach lurches out of sight with parents wiping away their tears, the children begin to open comics, don headphones, play cards, abuse the drivers of cars, everything but spare a thought for the weeping men and women they've left behind.

The callousness of youth towards age is never more marked than this.

Unpacking

The sensible and well-organised teachers will have a system for this procedure and for weeks beforehand children will have been forced to practice their unpacking during games lessons. Most teachers, however, seem prepared to put up with being unprepared, to suffer a free for all, wandering from room to room through blizzards of clothing and cuddly toys. After travelling and the pleasantries associated with arrival, unpacking takes up the rest of the first day. It's usually followed by a meal of fishfingers, mashed potatoes and beans.

Discovery

On the second day, the major discoveries are made. For example, most outward-bound activity centres have considerable open spaces attached to them, and this acreage is ripe for exploration. It will often contain tyre swings, treehouses, rope bridges and bands of frightened small animals that, on seeing children, are genetically disposed to run.

Children display a territoriality to their new-found surroundings, marking tree trunks and any brick surfaces with crude symbols or mis-spelled names, followed by the date to place themselves in a historical context.

Some steal things too. Normally smaller items are favoured, such as tools left lying around by farmers or the odd wellington boot. On occasion, larger implements have gone missing. In Lincolnshire, at the Juniper Berry Oast House Centre for the Nominally Disenfranchised, a local farmer complained when an entire herd of Friesian cattle was transported from a field, only to be found, hours later, in a coach park in Boston. There was much talk of children being 'sent home' and many threats of discipline being dished out on the groups' return to school. But no one owned up. Trevor Hutchcroft was suspected by the Centre Manager, but it was never proven beyond reasonable doubt.

A Class Act

Mud

A special factor, this one. Slurry, brown primeval ooze, manure, swampturf, quicksand, call it what you will, these substances which elsewhere might just be picked up on the soles of your shoe will, in these environs, cover every item of clothing, and constitute a large percentage of belly button fluff. Mud will infiltrate your nostrils, your eyes and your ears. It is a ubiquitous ingredient in any residential trip recipe.

Try this test. Look at the photographs that form part of the necessary school exhibition four weeks after your return. Recognising your pupils is difficult. The thick veneer of earthy rheum obscures their features. You yourself are only identifiable by virtue of your height. Every one of the humans represented in the pictures is a murky, encrusted sub-species of British Sasquatch. Canary yellow, mid-atlantic, storm-proof coats are rendered invisible by the thick coating of semi-liquid clay and earth. It's as if you and your kind have been rolling around in the stuff.

Which is, of course, exactly what you have been doing.

There is an urge to run headlong into fields of mud which seems to grip everybody on residential trips. Indeed, the degenerate behaviour of children en-masse, as documented in *Lord of the Flies*, is observable on an annual basis up and down the country as groups of screaming children use sticks and stones to funnel their hapless teachers down towards the thickest, deepest, sulphuric pools of noxious ooze.

That teachers have internalised this process and see it as just another part of the week to be got through, is testimony to the fact that such goings on have been part of these trips since time immemorial. To see the look of resignation on the face of Mr. Thornton, as he is ritually herded down into the grimpen mire is to witness the inconsequence of man in the face of Darwinian theory. In the grandiose scheme of the residential trip, the place of mud is secure, and the right of children to pummel their pedagogues into the stuff is inalienable.

The Lost Boys

This nasty surprise is always sprung, but it's the joker in the pack, in that it can occur at any moment during the week, and is apt to reoccur, depending on the hand

A Class Act

fate deals you. One teacher's experience serves as an excellent example of the Lost Boys phenomenon. On a week's trip to a small Christian-based activity centre in Hampshire, Mr. Cheasly and his band of thirty eleven year-olds were on a day trip to Winchester Cathedral. The forty-one year old bachelor hoped that the sanctity of the building would subdue the bombastic tendencies of a small group of amateur electricians, four boys named Alf, Walt, Wilf and Freddy. How wrong he was. At exactly 1400 hours the cry went up: "Where's Alfie, sir?"

Scanning the group, he could see the boy was indeed absent. As were the other three members of his coterie. "Oh, Christ!" Mr. Cheasly sighed, much to the disgust of a passing bishop. "I knew I should have never unshackled them." And he pulled a nest of chains from his shoulder bag, then angrily tossed them down onto the tomb of Izzak Walton. "Right everyone, I want you to all sit here under this crucifix and you're not to move until I get back, okay?" The robotic chorus of assent rang out in the vast nave like a solemn 'Amen'. Beginning his search in the Cathedral shop, Mr. Cheasly moved among the tourists and pilgrims as laconically as possible. He wanted to avoid starting a panic, despite feeling distinctly frantic himself.

Walking into a display of postcards and sending several hundred laminated views of the West Front high into the air, he managed a garbled apology and asked if anyone had seen four young boys. The twitching faces of the elderly women behind the counter suggested to him that he ought to leave before they summoned the local constable. Down the aisles he roamed, softly cooing the names of the lost boys. Each one reverberated back to him a thousand times louder, echoing powerfully in the glassy stillness of the perpendicular arches. Several visitors took photographs of him. A tourist guide tried to set fire to him. Despite all of the attention, Mr. Cheasly trod, up to the Lady Chapel and in and out of the transepts. "Alf! Wilf! Walter! Frederick!"

After several hours of fruitless searching and with evensong about to commence, every visitor to the building was stilled by the announcement on the antiquated PA system. "At this hour every day we ask all those gathered here under this great and ancient vault to pause and to reflect on some contemporary issues of theological interest." All around the Cathedral people stood still and listened. "The weather pattern known as El Nino is wreaking havoc across the the world today. Here in Winchester we have a manifest example of this natural phenomena's awesome power. Recent high winds have taken many tiles from the roof and restoration is sorely needed. We would ask you to consider making a generous..."

But here the tannoy crackled, buzzed and the announcement by the Provost was replaced by the cackling sound of childrens' laughter. Then the scratched intro to a

A Class Act

well known rap number filled the air. Up in the bell tower, ensconced from the world below, the four missing pupils had set up a pirate radio station using three old coat hangers and a bucket of sand. They spent the rest of the evening singing Abba songs and telling irreverent stories about Mr. Cheasly.

Even after they had been found, driven from their hiding place by the local fire brigade and successfully returned to Cheasly's flock, they were considered 'spiritually lost' by the local parishioners who, up until this day, remember the whole episode with rancour and bitterness. 'Cheasly' has become a byword for Satan in the city of Winchester.

Homesickness

It is not just teachers who cry miserably into their pillows each night, wailing bitterly for their mothers and fathers. Children have been known to do this too. In the dead of night, sometimes for the duration of the trip, tormented dreams of home-cooking and the smell of the dustpan and brush seep into the somnambulant brains of the children and they yell out in despair, wanting more than anything else to be home. The teacher's role in such situations is clearly defined. Spend fifteen minutes softly whispering words of comfort in the hope that the errant youth will drift back into the land of nod; if this fails, bark the command "GO TO SLEEP" as viciously as possible. This will, in all probability, wake up the entire dormitory, but they will at least be silent, quivering at the wrath of a sleep-deprived adult, with a mixture of fear and loathing usually reserved for playground bullies or East European dictators.

Pocket Money

To be confiscated at the earliest opportunity, with only a fraction of the original sums returned to individuals whilst in a small gift shop that stocks nothing more than pencils, sharpeners and bars of pink nougat. The surplus to be creamed off and invested in three or four extra bottles of wine to aid relaxation at the end of a gruelling day.

Food

It was during a week long trip to Weston-Super-Mare as a young boy that Lionel Bart first struck upon the idea of turning Oliver Twist into a musical. As he and his

A Class Act

friends awaited breakfast on their second morning at the High Grange Correctional Centre for the Emotionally Bereft (kippers and porridge, a combination universally hated by them all under normal circumstances) they were overcome by an urge to leap on top of the trestle tables and sing ancient farming songs. In fact, before every meal they were so excited by the imminent arrival of their food that young Lionel decided to pen a melody to the victuals on offer. Meals on residential trips are little peaks of excitement each day.

There is no earthly reason why this should be so. Yet it is an unassailable fact that at 8.00am, 12.00pm and 6.00pm a frenzy of anticipation sweeps through the bodies of staff and children like a broom through a dark passageway. Nobody has discovered whether this is due to the monotony associated with country pursuits or because everyone feels a compulsion to look hungry and appreciative. Whatever the cause, you see a ripple of pleasure convulse around the communal dining area as the fragrance of mince, chips and peas wafts its way to freedom through the unfeasonably lengthy serving hatch.

The Return Journey

The journey home is a celebratory affair. Weighed down with pencils, sharpeners, bars of pink nougat and brass rubbings, the children begin to sing songs and generally make merry. Some have been known to spontaneously combust, such is their excitement at the thought of returning home. Teachers feel euphoric at this point. It's as if the holidays have begun. Many are gripped by the urge to run into stationary shops and buy every red pen in the place. Others simply begin speaking fluent Spanish while strumming an imaginary flamenco guitar.

Parties have been thrown by returning teachers which have caused traffic problems on the Esher by-pass. The Red arrows sometimes voluntarily fly overhead before skywriting 'Wilcom Hom' (e's are tricky). In the evening as the teachers slip between the sheets of their own beds, they will let out sighs of relief and regret. Relief because they have all of their limbs intact and can remember the name of the current Prime Minister. Regret because the croaking and clucking emanating from their unpacked suitcases suggests that a number of birds and animals have been secreted between the balled up socks and T-shirts for their general edification and amusement. It is with a heavy heart and an imaginative excuse that they pick up their telephones and dial the number for the RSPCA.

A Class Act

14. *The Pot Noodle as a Luxury Item*

Teachers and money

Teachers are not driven by money. In fact, they tend to begin their careers thankful for receiving any payment that amounts to more than a grant. In the first few years of a teaching career, by way of incremental salary points granted each September, teachers find their pay packets steadily fattening. These financial fillips distract their attention enough for them not to notice that, despite being paid more every twelve months, they still earn less than everybody else in the industrialised world.

As if to add insult to injury, one fine September morning they discover, to their utter dismay, that there is no new incremental point for the forthcoming year. This is because they have reached the lowly heights of the pay ceiling, whereby they can earn no more by dint of classroom teaching alone. Sure, if they want to take on further responsibilities and hassle, they can earn a little extra, but many have no room in their day for added tasks. Even though each day spent in a school adds to one's skills and ability, someone in a grey office, a long time ago, decided that such a pay ceiling would exist. Thus, a teacher with seven years experience earns exactly the same amount as a teacher with thirty-seven years experience. This is not only a paradox, but a disgrace in the modern workplace. Whilst those in other careers move, progress and advance, teachers stand still.

The present Labour administration has admitted that the issue of pay does pose a problem for recruitment and retention. The government's proposal is to create a new pay scale for classroom teachers whereby a selection by dint of appraisal would cross a 'threshold', and move onto a higher pay scale whilst still remaining a classroom practitioner. In addition a tiny portion of teachers would become advanced skills teachers, with a new set of responsibilities. These advanced skills, or exemplary teachers, would then be able to share good practice with colleagues and help in the drive to raise standards. Many in the profession have criticised these proposals for being divisive. They claim that the selection of these people would be subjective and would affect the strong teamwork ethos in schools.

In responding to this criticism, those who support such a scheme point out that many in a school do already earn differing sums of money. Those with allowances for extra tasks earn more. However the difficulty with the new threshold proposals is that within a school a handful of people would be paid more than their colleagues whilst remaining classroom teachers. Yes, they would cross the threshold as a result of successful appraisal, but many may feel that their additional work would not

A Class Act

justify the quite considerable pay differential.

The real problem is that with nearly half a million teachers in this country, an across the board pay increase would add a massive digital deluge on the treasury's annual bill. Treasury officials do not like this and will not stand for it. Therefore in reality what will happen is that a selection of the profession will move onto the new pay scale whilst a sizable proportion will stay behind on the old ceiling-limited grading.

The salary

It is interesting to note that in teacher recruitment advertising, the salary is usually not promoted in upper case letters, for fear of inciting ribald laughter. In fact, better to avoid the subject of salary altogether. In the now infamous Teacher Training Agency cinema advert, a host of celebrities lined up to simply say the name of their best teacher. "Miss Tubbs", "Eric Anderson", "Mr. Lipscombe". If they had instead mouthed, "Fourteen thousand three hundred pounds" the effect on receptive audiences would have been markedly different. After the snorts of derision had subsided, people would have turned to the friend or stranger sitting next to them and made a lifelong committment to a career in taxidermy.

There are no "attractive packages" in teaching recruitment adverts, nor are there "competitive bonuses". You could look for, but would not find: company cars, free private medical insurance, profit-share schemes, sports facilities or complimentary gluten-free health products. But there are some benefits. On the plus side, the salary is regular. As far as money is concerned, that's about it. Non-financial reasons are often cited as incentives to become a teacher. Like nurses, teachers are expected to always give more than they get. They are paid "in kind," by seeing their charges grow up to be good citizens and upstanding members of their local communities.

Every teacher harbours secret ambitions to nurture a future nobel-prize winner or Olympic athlete. Teachers are told that the satisfaction of enabling a child to read is worth all of the money in the world. As retired teachers, huddled around one bar of a faulty electric fire will tell you, none of this counts for very much, and many in the profession would gladly sacrifice the nation's literacy for an extra tenner a month and a packet of cheesy wotsits.

The starting salary is actually not that bad. From student days, spent existing on a diet of corned beef and tinned spaghetti, it is a joyous experience to visit Kwik-Save and purchase something resembling a weekly shop. In fact newly qualified teachers have been known to suffer from a condition known as 'supermarket rush'

A Class Act

- whereby the sheer shock of being able to take an item from each and every aisle, in the knowledge that they will be able to pay for them, leads to a drug-like euphoria which manifests itself in running around wildly and climbing into other people's trollies.

With money regularly siphoned into their bank accounts (however paltry the amounts may be), teachers immediately are consumers in the global chain of income and expenditure. And it is not just in the nation's supermarkets that their money is filtered away. Men and women of independent means they are not, but teachers must still stitch together a lifestyle of sorts.

Lifestyle Choices

i. *"Let's do lunch"*

Whilst the rest of the world consumes nouvelle cuisine from immaculate china platters - allowing droplets of purple elixir to delicately drizzle down their throats, teachers stare through the glass panel of a microwave, watching the contents of their soup bowl gyrate and splutter.

Staffroom fridges groan under the weight of super-value tubs of *St. Ivel Gold*, home-made sandwiches and milk cartons that are lapsing toward foul olfactory territory. Cupboards contain half-finished packets of stale *Ryvita*, sachets of *Cup-a-soup*, an assortment of gaudily decorated rice-cake packets, and the occasional soggy grape.

It is rare to see a three course meal served in a staffroom; it is commonplace to see the reheated scraps from last night's culinary effort. Lunch in a staffroom is definitely not a black-tie, silver service affair. A Marks and Spencer brocoli mornay is looked upon with envious glances and dreams of the high life. As exotic recipes are flicked through in *Sainsbury's* magazine, most know that in reality some pasta tubes infused with a tin of tomatoes is the nearest they'll ever get to Mediterranean excellence.

During holidays, teachers screen their incoming calls, so fearful are they of the possibility of being asked out to lunch. Afeared and yet strangely attracted. As the incoming message is being recorded, questions buzz inside their heads, such as what shall I wear, who will pay, and will there be cutlery? The prospect of a midday meal consumed in a public place is one fraught with spinach-between-the-teeth scenarios and stomach-rumbling embarrassments.

And yet, fuelled by a primal desire to rejoin an adult world, your holidaying

A Class Act

teacher cannot resist the temptation afforded by the offer of lunch for two at one of those brightly-lit brasseries. Once inside the eaterie, they spend tense moments, frantically reminding themselves not to blurt out "Wimpey and chips" to the expectant waiter. By looking around at eaters in the immediate vicinity, they are able to mirror the conventions of the dining table in much the same way a visiting martian would.

Growing in confidence, the teacher lets their guard down, and stops concentrating just long enough to suddenly find themselves irritated by the noise the chefs are making. Before their host can stop them, they begin marching towards the kitchens.

The stunned chefs gaze in awe and wonder, leaving the day's supply of bechamel sauce to congeal on the bottom of a cast-iron pan, as the double doors crash open, and a hoarse voice insists on silence. The teacher distributes several letters to be given out at the end of the day, and returns to their seat, blissfully unaware that the police have been called.

So much for dining out. What about the domestic eating habits of a teacher? Although the opportunity to expand one's culinary repertoire presents itself during the summer holidays, many teachers find they follow the impulse towards reconstituted packet lunches where the most technical kitchen appliance they need to utilise is a kettle. A baked potato with cheese is seen as a 'way out' dining experience, and if a tin of tuna is added to the equation, then visions of dancing on a Hawaiian beach are entertained.

Hot food is complemented by cold. Crisps, biscuits, chocolates and fig rolls supplement the microwaved fare, thereby ensuring the presence of at least one of the five major food groups. Calories do not abound, however, and it has been noted in a recent study at Loughborough University that a 'concertina' effect takes place among many teachers, whose quality of lunching goes up and down in line with Christmas, Easter and Summer holidays, resulting in a dramatic rise and fall in body fat percentages.

Poor nutritional content, although tasty, pulls teachers in a downward spiral towards ill-health, numerous colds and periods of moaning that would drive even the most patient of counselling students into a frenzied rage.

ii. *Motors*

From the environs of a staffroom, take a stroll to the space where the staff cars are haphazardly parked, and look for the trappings that adorn a wealth-encrusted

A Class Act

lifestyle. But wait, there is no sign of a B.M.W, no sighting of a Porsche with spoilers and sunroof, no glimpse of a Range-Rover with twin air-bags and mineral water dispenser. Instead, you will observe a selection of Fiat Uno's, battered Golfs and an array of Ford Fiestas.

The back seats of these vehicles will be piled high with unmarked books, crumpled worksheets and leaves that were intended for unworkable science experiments. Many of these cars have low-mileage and are fairly new but have undergone pre-emptory vandalism by their owners, in the sure knowledge that a battered and rusty old heap will be less likely to attract the defacements and amateur panel beatings of the regular attendees of the 'lunchtime detention club'. In addition, there is a high frequency of dead batteries in the after school hours, ensuring that many a school caretaker gets to practice their smug facial expressions and patronising put-downs.

Of course many of these mysterious 'school car park flat battery' scenarios are directly attributable to said caretakers, who, in a clandestine effort to force down electricity bills hook up twelve volt batteries to the school's ring main. Not only does this result in many calls to the AA, at a time when most self-respecting teachers are settling down to watch *Newsround*, but also accounts for the perennially feeble lighting in many of our school classrooms.

Teachers' cars have to be multi-modal, like the Indian Tri-shaw or the French farmer's Citroen, in that they serve more than one purpose and are utilised at the most unexpected of times. Not only are they required for transporting children to and from sporting fixtures, they are also needed as makeshift ambulances, ferriers of scrap-bank materials, and moto-cross substitutes.

iii. *Fashion*

Like most professions, the fashion range within the teaching community is vast. Some sport clothes of such fine cut and style, that entry to the land's most exclusive clubs would be automatically guaranteed, whilst others look like a torn refuse sack, without tie-handles. The debate on fashion has raged for some time now, but it has always taken place against a theoretical dilemma of how smart teachers should be for the classroom.

There is a strong school of thought which argues that teachers should be immaculately and formally turned out. This, it is reasoned, gives an impression of seriousness and maturity, and strengthens the childrens' respect for their instructors. However, to counter this, some ask, what's the point of being beautifully presented,

A Class Act

when in all likelihood you're going to be covered in ink marks and charcoal by the end of the day? Another group suggests that the more downtrodden you look, the better your teaching. In the maelstrom of a classroom, the scruffy teacher can concentrate on shaping enquiring minds, instead of skipping past falling glue containers, to avoid staining a recently purchased two-piece linen suit.

But clothes, food, motors and other consumables are dependent on an income, and as we have seen the credit column of a teacher is sad and pathetic looking next to its big debit brother. To increase one's spending ability, there are a range of extra-curricular money-making schemes that can be pursued.

Money-Making Schemes

a. Moonlighting

Sometimes, teachers do attempt to set up small businesses within their school. These have included: tuck-shops, alternative canteens, bicycle cleaning and maintenance, share-dealing services and anaesthetic-free dentistry. Almost all of these schemes end in financial ruin, with the initiators often being sued by parents of empy-pocketed, toothless children.

b. The Lottery

Our advice is simple: you have more chance of becoming a lizard than winning the lottery.

For other get-rich-quick scams try:

1. Betting.
2. Extortion.

c. Quiz Shows

If you are really desperate, the television quiz show offers a semi-realistic route to wealth and happiness. Teachers are well known as repositories of useless information, and would probably do well on *Mastermind* or *Fifteen-to-one*. But a terracotta bull and an imitation Grecian urn aren't the kind of rewards most teachers have in mind. A better choice would be any one of the many peak time mainstream

A Class Act

quiz shows offering big cash prizes and a twenty foot boat with trailer. To win one of these shows requires some planning on the part of the teacher. This usually consists of regular two-hour stints on the local pub's trivia machine.

With the arrival of *Who Wants To Be A Millionaire?*, teachers do have a decent chance of getting to sit in a baking television studio, with Chris Tarrant pulling pained faces at you. The idea behind this particular programme is that millions of people ring a premium line quiz number and answer some questions. A tiny percentage of those who answer correctly, are eventually selected to appear on the show.

Each programme has ten of these 'lucky' souls battling it out with each other for the right to sit in the hot seat. In order to achieve this, you need to put four items in a 'correct order', for example *place four types of wheat cracker in weight order, starting with the lightest one first*. The contestant who achieves this feat in the quickest time moves forward to sit near Mr. Tarrant, and answers a range of increasingly complex multiple choice questions. In this respect, *Who Wants To Be A Millionaire?*, does bear some resemblance to what is currently going on in the nation's classrooms. This should give teachers an advantage.

The tests which children are expected to sit, do contain questions which get more difficult as the papers progress. There is an element of multiple choice in some of the tests. Therefore, it can be reasoned that if Mr. Tarrant could be persuaded, future tests could be conducted by live satellite link-up's, with his royal gameshowness asking the questions, and a menacing electronic soundtrack humming in the background. This method would not ensure better test results, but it would make the whole enterprise more entertaining.

d. Loans

APR.
Preferential interest rates.
Base rates.
Cash-back.
Consolidation.
Fixed-rate.
Credit facility.
Payment protection.
Terms and conditions.

A Class Act

These are just some of the many bullets teachers have to dodge when they enter the battlefield of personal loans. However, although the brochures advertising loans are glossy and enticing, one fact above all others remains. It's not your money. Somebody's lent it to you. And you have to pay it back.

A Class Act

15. *Bring back the ducking stool*

Why teachers are made scapegoats for all of society's ills

At the end of the school day Angela Rathbone (aged fifty-seven) reclines in her comfortable classroom chair, and thinks back to the golden days that reigned **Before Vilification (BV)**...

In those far-off times she enjoyed the finest years of a blossoming teaching career, with her youth forming but one small part of the equation. In that segment of history, she had experienced a freedom to organise her classroom in a way she saw fit - a freedom that in turn liberated her pupils to explore and discover all manner of knowledge and skills.

Of course there were documents to be completed and education ministry directives to be followed, but she was granted a respect both by the government and the public. This made her modest wage seem less important, and filled her with a sense of purpose and pleasure. She not only felt she was making a contribution to society, everyone else was forever reminding her.

It is with a start that she wakes from her reverie, to face the cold light of the present, and sits bolt upright, as her Headteacher raps on the display-laden classroom window wearily waving the latest tome of governmental commands to be shot onto the desks of every teacher in the country.

Angela glances from the threatening hardbacked file in the Head's grasp to the towering mountain of forms on her desk, and her warm vision of the old days recedes into the misty background. *How can it be*, she wonders, as she sips from a mug of lukewarm tea, *that as a teacher, I have gone from being one of the most celebrated and lauded of public servants, to being on the receiving end of a barrage of insults and accusations?*

The Press Factor

'Trendy teaching methods are failing our children'.

'Teachers refuse to teach baa baa black sheep.'

'Loony left lessons on lesbian lego.'

These were the types of headlines that became daily fare in the late seventies and

A Class Act

early eighties. Story after story pounded onto the nation's breakfast tables, as teachers were harangued from all quarters. Gone were the 'feel good' pieces about endearing teachers and fascinating classroom achievements. Instead there appeared a series of increasingly hysterical articles, from both tabloid and broadsheet papers.

From the mighty nationals to the backwater minnows, teachers were singled out as the profession whose bell was tolling. The accumulation of harshly critical articles created a climate whereby it was common practice to attack the profession. It became an accepted wisdom among certain sections of the press that teachers had been hiding behind a facade of incompetence and complacency for too long. Teaching methods were questioned. Teachers' political opinions were examined. Classes and assemblies were visited by scavenging reporters. Highly vituperative editorials were penned. Thus today, after twenty years of critical opinion heaped upon the profession, we are no longer shocked by the type of opinion piece headline appearing in the Daily Telegraph (17/12/98); *'The teachers' plot to make our children into failures.'*

We are often reminded that in a nation which boasts a free press, negative stories are far more interesting than their positive counterparts, and we shall now see how even an episode of promise and harmony can be transformed into a bleak morality tale.

Picture if you will...

A school in the Midlands has just been granted a glowing Ofsted report. The staff are unwinding beneath the tantalising halo of praise dressed up in official clothing, and Janice, the Headteacher, is pogoing madly in the hall to the sounds of a T-Rex number. Chart tunes blare from the ancient music-system in the welfare-assistant's cubby-hole, and the caretaker is giving people rides along the corridor in his wheelbarrow.

The phone rings in the staffroom, and an elated Adrienne, the maths coordinator, leaps for the receiver, completing a mid-air somersault whilst relishing the chance to perform another few bars of *'Yessir I can boogie.'*

It is Brian Fox, a gentleman from the local newspaper, who wants some furtive gleanings from the as yet, unpublished findings of the Ofsted team. Adrienne knows that the staff have been told to keep the great tidings to themselves, but something intoxicating in the atmosphere and the half bottle of sparkling white wine she has consumed, make her open to questioning. She screams ecstatically

A Class Act

into the receiver about how well the maths section is going to look and details a host of other triumphs.

When asked if there are any fault lines, Adrienne hesitates, but does mention that although geography was generally upheld to be well-taught in the school, not enough time was devoted to it during the inspection week. Slamming down the phone and rejoining the enormously tangled bundle in the middle of the staffroom carpet, she instantaneously forgets all about this call.

Two days later, the local paper thuds onto the secretary's desk with the volatile explosiveness of a homemade molotov cocktail. SCHOOL FAILING AT GEOGRAPHY, yells the banner headline, and as the newsprint edges into the staffroom, a terrible vision returns to haunt Adrienne, who is so abjectly guilty of the leak. Toying agonisingly over what to do, as all around her start chanting ancient war rites, she solemnly announces to the entire staff group that it was she who blabbed. They are extremely tolerant of her foolhardy flittishness, apart from the geography co-ordinator who puts an ancient curse on her. Adrienne promises not to answer the staffroom phone ever again.

The Headteacher in an attempt at damage limitation, approaches the newspaper in question, explaining to the news editor, calmly but forcefully that the blip in geography is inconsequential in the light of the overall report. The Head explains that the full report will be almost universal in its praise of the school, and that the inspectors were delighted with what they had seen. Having ostensibly cleared the matter up, the Head returns to her busy schedule and puts the matter out of her mind. The paper's front page headline the following week is, HEAD DEFENDS SCHOOL'S FAILURE AT GEOGRAPHY.

The Head is now furious and demands a meeting with the paper's editor. He, a besuited world-weary campaigner in his late forties with a hairstyle straight out of *Hawaii-Five-O*, grants her some of his time, and listens with a bored expression to her rantings for fifteen minutes. Her comments are dutifully reported the following week in two paragraphs on page thirteen, beside an advertorial piece about a new restaurant specialising in crab dishes.

This ability to change a positive piece of news from, SCHOOL ACHIEVES EXCELLENCE IN GOVERNMENT INSPECTION to SCHOOL FAILING AT GEOGRAPHY demonstrates the manner in which good news about a school is trampled over in the hunt for even the smallest particle of dirt. It has led many to conclude that unless vast sums of money are offered or the school has total editorial control over a piece, one should be extremely vigilant when dealing with the local press.

A Class Act

The national press works on similar principles, but naturally the stories are of a wider significance. The national papers have put a huge amount of time and resources into covering the education debate in this country over the last two decades. Each paper has its own identity and agenda with regard to this issue. Whilst sections of the press feel they should construct some form of defence for teachers, they have often been too weak in the face of monolithic directives and research provided by successive administrations.

Even the more liberal sections of the press who can number many thousands of teachers amongst their readership, do not always make a sufficient defence of, and advocacy for the teaching profession.

The Broadcast media presents a mixed picture. BBC coverage, being balanced and a little bland, ITV's, racey and impertinent, Channel 4's, hushed and serious and Channel 5's, well we don't know, because we've never managed to get a decent picture. The news on the ITV network does sometimes carry a lighthearted teaching item in its 'and finally' section, but tales of schools that double up as night bakeries, or teachers who cross dress for P.E lessons are hardly likely to affect the national debate on the state of our nation's schools.

The proliferation of radio channels means that you can hear just about every type of music, should you so desire, and a host of differing news formats. The *Today* programme on Radio 4 has consistently covered teaching stories in depth with a degree of panache and commitment, and if you like to tune in to a good old barny, then this is your programme. The independent networks do feature some interesting school-based pieces, but adverts about local fish superstores have to be endured in the breaks.

You don't require a diploma in Media Studies to see that the press, radio and TV are far from being steadfast allies of the teaching profession. But to prove this point unequivocally we invite you to participate in a small-scale experiement.

Choose a week, any week, don't show it to us, and put it back in the pack. During this chosen seven day period, buy a selection of newspapers and cut out every article that features schools, teachers, or educational standards in any way. Arrange these in front of you on a table. Pin them up on a noticeboard. Make doilies out of them. Whatever means of studying them you choose, take a little time to read them, re-read them, and to compare their headlines, content and overall tone.

Looking at these nuggets in detail you will get a feel for the slant of each piece. It is likely that you will notice an underlying trend that links each article together. Teachers are failing. From cheating Headteachers who open exam papers too early, to classroom teachers who are too soft on unruly pupils. From children who can't

A Class Act

spell properly, to governing bodies that are too lenient on poor teaching. Put together, these numerous articles provide a collective picture of a teaching world in crisis. They say in loud and accusatory tones, there is something very amiss with schools in this country, and even after years of pressure and threats, the problems are still fundamentally there.

In the playground of life, the press are the hulking bullies and teachers are the weedy victims of their mindless attacks. But are these attacks truly mindless or is it the case that the teacher as public enemy number one scenario was sketched out some years ago during a time of great political and social upheaval.

The Political Factor

BV, it was social workers who bore the brunt of cynical attacks, being condemned for wearing colourful waistcoats and making their voices turn higher and inquisitive at the end of every sentence. Studying historical archives, it is quite easy to spot that the 'anti-teacher' culture is a relatively modern phenomenon. Not as modern as the internet, but more contemporary than the rationing of butter. Teachers do not sit untarnished in the wastebasket of newspaper history, but before the nineteen-sixties, they were often praised, sometimes commended and at times even celebrated.

Of course there were instances where a certain individual or institution had been found wanting in one way or another, but these episodes were not part of any coherent campaign, and there was no evidence of a pervading negative culture in relation to the profession. With the arrival in this country of new educational methods, (which skipped onto these shores arm in arm with self-help books and yoga summer camps from the U.S.A.) there was every possibility that teachers who embraced such techniques would be in for a hard time.

In some quarters the dirt was duly dished out, and a variety of insults were levelled at teachers, ranging from, *why aren't this lot teaching my children anything of value?* to *I refuse to have my child listening to cassette recordings of performing wheat.*

Throughout the sixties and seventies, these hissings of discontent simmered in the papers and there were sporadic attacks on 'progressive' teaching methods. Whilst some in the profession did entertain a portion of these American inventions, by changing their name to 'Essence' or dressing in herb sachets, many distanced themselves in much the same way as a builder strays from their original quote. Traditionalists stuck quite rigidly to the ways they knew best - the teaching of

A Class Act

phonics, times tables and handwriting schemes.

The overall regard for the profession remained very high in this period of political and cultural change, and in annual surveys teachers were always near the pinnacle in the league of the nation's most-respected work groupings. However, as the seventies drew to a close, their were signs of a 'get tough' approach from the Callaghan administration, and then the Conservative party started to win the P.R. offensive, striding past the post at the general election of 1979.

Margaret Thatcher and her cohorts settled into their new offices, and almost immediately started to run amok in Westminster like a gang of naughty children let loose in a sweet shop in the depths of the night. They ploughed through as much of the liberal/public sector ancien regime as they could, promoting free enterprise, the rights of the individual and the destruction of the unions.

Conservative strategists from Mrs. T downwards argued that an agenda must be set for the coming decades of Conservative rule, which would pluck the nation from obscurity and make Britain great again. Socialism was the creed of the envious and if it had its way would turn Britain into a Russian outpost. Liberalism was beyond half-baked, with its sandal wearers and compromisers who would dearly love to sell Britain out to the menace of the European Union. No, the nation's future had been entrusted to Margaret and her henchpeople, and if it meant becoming the most unpopular administration in this country since records were started, then that was a price well worth paying.

We're out to get you

It soon became clear that teachers did not fit comfortably into the Conservative master plan. After all, here were a bunch of liberal-leaning characters, who by the very nature of their job worked in a collective spirit and as part of a small community. Something would have to be done about them she insisted. Their teaching styles and their open-mindedness were brazen insults to all that was dear to the Tory hierarchy. If these so-called 'professionals' would not comply with their wishes, then the Conservatives would (market) force them to do so. Teachers were facing one of the most drawn out battles any profession has ever experienced.

As the Conservative government argued for less centralised control whilst simultaneously spreading their power across the country, 'Quango' replaced 'Tango' as one of the nation's favourite advertising slogans. Stories began to appear in the press that gave a hint of what was to follow. Mrs. Thatcher was advised by her commanders in their think-tanks that standards in school were at an all time low,

A Class Act

and under a ridiculously liberal and confused Labour administration had been plummeting for years. Gone were the rigour and discipline from days of old, in was children sitting in groups, chatting about pop music and not doing any sums. Teachers were getting kids to talk about feelings instead of Shakespeare, and standard English was being allowed to float out of the classroom window to make way for some modern multicultural T.V. dialect.

As some of the mud began to stick, teachers gradually developed a siege mentality, trying to get on with their daily tasks whilst continually being reminded that they were beneath a cloud of shame, as if a disapproving uncle was always hovering nearby. They were warned implicitly that not only was their card marked, but that if they did not make amends for previous misbehaviour, they might just find themselves in the ever lengthening queues at the dole office. This climate of bitterness and suspicion crystallised some years later in the formation of the Office for Standards in Education.

The Ofsted Factor

Ofsted was not set up when Margaret Thatcher was Prime Minister, although many attribute its existence to her revolutionary zeal with regard to all things educational. It was established during the premiership of John Major as a non-governmental department. Ofsted's remit was to inspect and monitor standards in schools. Its hidden agenda (although this soon became very public) was to shake up the supposed complacency within the teaching profession, and to sound the death knell for the progressive practitioners. Its aim was to provide a rolling programme of inspection for every state school in England, pointing out areas of weakness while also singling out areas of good practice. It was in 1994 that Christopher Woodhead was appointed to lead Ofsted under the title Her Majesty's Chief Inspector Of Schools.

The Demon or the Demonised

At times it is quite possible to forget what the purpose of the Office for Standards In Education actually is, because so much press coverage is about Mr. Woodhead himself. Thousands of words have been penned portraying him as evil, many others have noted his saintly qualities. The core of his basic premise is that standards of education in this country have been falling over a period of years due in part to

A Class Act

'trendy teachers.' By this he means teachers who dare to stray away from the steady reliability of whole-class teaching, chalk and talk and the three 'r's.

According to his master plan, there is a correct way of doing things in the classroom. He insists that a sizable proportion of the teaching profession in their stubbornness and lack of vision refuse to take on board all of his findings and those of his inspection teams. So where does he get the notion that standards have been falling and that large numbers of teachers through their slavish devotion to basket-weaving and finger-painting are preventing children's progress? This is a difficult question to answer.

There is no clear reliable body of evidence that points unequivocally to declining reading and writing standards in this country. Yet there are scores of lay people and academics who claim that children read less well now than was the case 'in their day'. This opinion is based, it seems, on nothing more substantive than 'commonsense'. Ask one of these people "how do you know standards have fallen?" and you invariably receive an anecdotal answer - "my nephew read to me the other day. It was a book with pictures and hardly any text. When I was his age I was reading Oliver Twist." What can we deduce from this? That children are reading less well now than they were twenty years ago? Or, that within the realm of education, arguments can be tossed around, with hugely diverse statistics being proffered by different interested parties?

Mr. Woodhead has stated that there are in the region of fifteen thousand teachers who are not up to the job. When he first made this claim, he explained, and has continued to explain that this figure was 'an extrapolation - the result of a statistical model.' Many teachers and union leaders were furious when Mr. Woodhead originally made these claims. *Where was the hard evidence?* they demanded. *Give us facts and figures not 'statistical models,'* they insisted. However, Mr. Woodhead was quick to point out that such extrapolations are commonly used in the field of research, and that it would be wrong of him not to report his initial findings.

This is a strategy often used by Mr. Woodhead. He uses 'extrapolations' to report *tendencies* and *trends* which highlight weaknesses in the profession. Yes, he may then follow these up with his inspection teams' 'hard evidence' to support his positions, but invariably the damage has often been done already. Perhaps the public release of these *trends* or *tendencies* is not such a good idea, especially as with the case of 'incompetent teachers' it caused so much anger within teaching circles. Teachers are not scared of the truth. It is just that many of them would prefer to always have the full evidence in front of them instead of 'extrapolations' and 'statistical models.' Whilst he releases his findings to the press, he places

A Class Act

responsibility for alarmist headlines at the door of newspaper editors. Does he not realise that the newspapers will pounce on his pronouncements with alacrity, focusing on the sensationalist aspects and ignoring the more pedestrian content? He could offer them forty pages of praise and one tentative paragraph containing the bombshell of 'fifteen thousand incompetent teachers' and we know what the headlines would be the next day. He must bear some of the responsibility for this.

Mr. Woodhead has made it clear that protecting teachers' feelings is not at the top of his agenda. He maintains he is primarily interested in higher standards being achieved in the nation's classrooms.

In all of this, he has missed a fundamental point. He needs teachers on his side, and whilst he may think his PR is sophisticated and successful, and claims that the majority of teachers who meet him are not antagonistic towards him, there are many within schools who believe that he is not good for the profession. This is not because teachers on the whole are a cynical, finger-wagging bunch of territory-defenders. They are in fact, generally, a decent open-minded assortment of people, as characteristic a cross-section of the populace as you're likely to find in any profession. But they do read newspapers and they do listen to the radio.

They have read and heard the criticisms he has made of the profession and are understandably aggrieved that the complexities of their career should be so crudely simplified in an Ofsted soundbite. Yet in spite of all this, Mr. Woodhead insists that his opponents 'demonise' him, because it is the only way they can challenge his arguments. He claims that they cannot defeat his reasoning so they try and transform him into cartoon-strip figure of hate. Many interest groups do indeed have a hate figure - a caricature, whose photo adorns office walls with obscenities gratuitously scrawled upon it. For the Left, Margaret Thatcher presented the perfect Diablo, and since her successors have offered little or no personal charisma, she has remained, for many, the epicentre of all that is capitalist and shameful.

In teaching, Mr. Woodhead has assumed the enemy's mantle. At times the battle between him and teachers resembles a playground name-calling exercise:

"You're demonising me."

"No you're demonising us."

"Well you did it first."

"Takes a demon to know a demon."

A Class Act

Yet there are some other extremely potent criticisms of Christopher Woodhead and Ofsted.

After years of schools in advantaged areas receiving better Ofsted reports than schools in disadvantaged areas, all that has changed is that the schools with the consistently higher standards will benefit from 'lighter touch' inspections, whilst the poorer performers will continue with the presumably 'heavy touch' regime. Mr. Woodhead continually maintains that less well-off schools can achieve excellent results, but has refused to properly tackle the thorny issue of 'context' in relation to his inspection teams' findings.

In the world of education, context is something you can ill-afford to ignore. Teachers have to understand the social background of their pupils if they are to make educational inroads. Not every child is the same. Not every school is the same. Therefore, the rigour of the Ofsted framework for inspection is illusory. You cannot drop the same framework onto radically different schools without fully taking into account their wider contexts. This doesn't mean that schools in disadvantaged areas are not expected to achieve success and fulfil children's potentials.

Every good teacher expects success. But Ofsted reports, which could provide an invaluable snapshot of the possible links between educational attainment and wider social factors, instead offer summaries of schools' achievements in a social vacuum. This begs the question, *what do Ofsted reports offer to schools and how do standards change post-inspection?*

If the comparisons between the education systems of England, Scotland and Wales are in any way indicative, then the answer would seem to be, not much. The GCSE results in England, Scotland and Wales have remained almost identical since Ofsted's inception. Neither Scotland nor Wales have the rigorous inspection regime favoured by Ofsted and yet exam results remain comparable. Mr. Woodhead and Ofsted can hardly be said, therefore, to be providing good value for money.

Where is the value in providing reports that are in no way developmental? Inspection reports provide little more than snapshot pictures of a few harassed days in a school's life. On the whole, neither inspectors nor their findings meet teachers half-way in a meaningful dialogue that seeks to improve a school. Instead their function is to drop a metaphorical bomb on failure and leave teachers to pick their way unaided through the rubble. However, Mr. Woodhead continues to contend that the inspection process does offer the opportunity for improvement in England's schools. Yet when faced with the unfavourable comparisons with non-Ofsted education systems elsewhere he backtracks and claims that Ofsted can only offer

A Class Act

advice and guidance.

When we interviewed him he said that it is not the remit of Ofsted to improve standards. He insists it is teachers who must act upon the advice of Ofsted reports in order to improve schools. Therein lies the problem: if Mr. Woodhead's rationale is based upon the premise that you can lead a horse to water but you can't force it to drink, then by implication he is suggesting that the intransigence of teachers is the deciding factor in any lack of improvement in SATs or exam results. This effectively means that Mr. Woodhead has engineered a win-win PR situation for himself with the blessing of consecutive governments. If standards improve Oftsted will take the lion's share of the praise, if they do not improve it is the fault of teachers.

As a result, in the eyes of teachers, he has become a sort of pedagogic Iago, waiting to turn his knife into the back of a defenceless Othello he has manipulated and ultimately betrayed. There have been protests, letters, petitions, depositions and all manner of complaining about him, but somehow he continually escapes from censure.

There is no concerted teacher-led conspiracy against him. It is simply that his combative style, critical outlook in the name of improving standards, and his use of the media have made him few friends in the nation's schools. However he likes to look at it, the overwhelming majority of teachers would welcome a new face at the Office for Standards in Education and the chance to work in an atmosphere of partnership and cooperation.

His management skills can also be called into question. Anyone involved in personnel management will tell you, that one needs to develop a positive work ethic based on mutual respect. The alienation of teachers continues to present him with a considerable barrier to progress, and one that he has shown little sign of doing anything about. He must surely, start to realise at some stage, that his PR needs to become far more positive towards the profession, in the very near future.

And this leaves us...where?

The Conservatives had eighteen years to destroy the morale of teachers in this country. Harnessing every press and publicity trick in the book, teachers were turned from dutiful servants to revolutionary traitors. For many of even the most mild-mannered or apolitical pedagogues, successive Conservative administrations were seen as an insult to the profession. When the Conservatives were crushed in the general election of 1997, many banked on there being a radical shake-up in the

A Class Act

education world.

The received wisdom was that Labour would embrace teachers, and whilst identifying paths for improvements would heap encouragement and praise onto all those who had suffered so miserably under Margaret's tirades. Unfortunately, the 'Let's blame teachers' mentality has in part survived the demise of the Conservatives, and to the consternation of many has found new life under new Labour. There are clearly some very senior politicians in this country who are dedicated to improving education in this country. They have made this very clear and have acted on some of their promises.

However, there does remain a major worry, that teachers are still viewed by some in government, as a group who still need to be pushed, and pushed quite forcefully. The tone may be softer than in the days of the Conservatives, and the press releases more sweetly written, but in truth, teachers are still routinely scolded for inconsistencies and incompetence. The negative press continues to give coverage to the political football that education has become. Most significantly of all, the Ofsted inspection regime remains in place.

Is change a possibility?

For those who joined the profession at any time since the start of the first Thatcher administration, being attacked is a part of one's daily routine, in much the same way as taking your class register or sitting on low brown chairs in the staffroom. Those who have graced the profession for a longer time, are in many cases still reeling from the initial shock of being singled out for status assassination. Talk to any teacher whose career spans twenty years or more and you will get a small insight into what life was truly like Before Vilification. Their words are a remarkable testimony to those golden years before anyone even dreamed of a concerted campaign against teachers.

Generally, teachers do feel a very real sense of being 'under attack' and their emotions cover anger, bitterness, frustration and despair. This is not because teachers are irrationally defensive. Of course there are problems in schools. It is impossible to visit any school, or for that matter any business, charity organisation, or other workplace and not find issues that need addressing. From the sharpest-shooting multinational conglomerate to the tiniest flower stall, there will be glitches that need ironing out. In the first instance, hiring a top new chief executive with a sixteen metre c.v may do the trick. In the latter, some plant bio food may be all that is required. Whatever the case, there will be gaps to be filled and questions to be

A Class Act

answered. That is the nature of our very existence. Perfection is not a reality, and those who spend too much time chasing it, are bitterly disappointed.

There are issues concerning teaching methods, training, discipline, levels of support, professionalism, but if you visit most schools in this country you will be struck by the level of staff commitment, the amount of satisfactory or good work produced and the bonds that exist between various sections of the school community. Schools on the whole are hugely positive places, where much learning and progress is made, and where massive strides are taken to improve educational standards and provide a safe and enjoyable atmosphere in which children can learn.

The profession has been losing the public relations battle for far too long. Teachers have been sold woefully short, and have been shaped into scapegoats for many of the nation's ills. This two-dimensional view of teachers and teaching is the biggest impediment to change.

If change is to become more than a dream, then governments, whatever their position on the political spectrum, and the press, whatever their political affliations, need to recognise that education is too fundamental to be constantly reviewed and monitored with one eye on voting behaviour. There are only so many changes teachers can embrace. There are only so many initiatives teachers can introduce into their classrooms.

Schools need to be seen as institutions above the vagaries of party politics. This is not to say that schools and teachers are exempt from criticism. Of course, some schools are not up to scratch, but heaping countless heavy handed inspection visits upon them is clearly not a humane or effective method of engendering improvement. There are equally teachers who need much guidance and support in order to improve.

The current climate of negativity is not the way forward.

It is time for politicians, newspaper editors and the Chief Inspector of Education to stop following their perception of public opinion and to start acting with a sense of responsibility rather than opportunism.

Things can change.

For proof of this look no further than the way in which teachers have incorporated the incredible amounts of legislative changes within schools since 1988 with, by and large, a great deal of success.

A Class Act

Teachers have repeatedly demonstrated their flexibility.

It is now the turn of other agencies to give a little.

A Class Act

16. Interview with Nigel de Gruchy

Nigel de Gruchy began his career, by teaching English as a foreign language teacher in Spain and France. He was Head of the Economics Department at St Joseph's Academy in the Inner London Education authority from 1968 to 1978. He took up a post as Assistant Secretary of the NASUWT in 1978, and in 1982 became the NASUWT's Deputy General Secretary. He has remained with the organisation ever since, becoming the union's General Secretary in 1990.

At the end of our interview with Nigel de Gruchy he asked us to join the NASUWT. This invitation demonstrates his committment to the organisation, which incidently has its headquarters above the Dr. Marten's shop in London's Covent Garden, an apt metaphor and one not lost on Conservative governments down the years. We had heard Mr. de Gruchy defending teachers on the radio at many junctures, both in those Conservative year's and during the days of the new Labour administration. We thought he would have words of wisdom to pass onto us.

JZ: To start off with - how much damage do you think successive Conservative governments did to the profession?

NdG: An enormous amount. It all began with the monetarism of Thatcher and Joseph in the early 1980's. They squeezed all public sector pay, and teachers suffered, provoking the inevitable response. There was a short dispute in 1984 which was quickly carted off to arbitration which was a good solution. And then in 1985 we got bogged down into a long dispute. There were mistakes made on both sides, but it stemmed from the government treating the public sector unfairly. That's what provoked it all. I'm not saying we couldn't have played things differently.

That then led to the big disputes of the mid 80's and to Thatcher wanting her retribution, not just with teachers, but their employers, the LEAs who she had good reason to believe were letting us run wild as a battering ram against the government. She determined to sort out not just the unions but the local authorities as well. She imposed an onerous contract which was the gateway through which anything could be thrown at teachers who were then expected to pick it up and run with it.

After that came the 1988 Education Reform Act which was mainly aimed at

A Class Act

destroying local authorities and the influence of unions. When you're motivated by a desire for retribution, as the Conservatives were, you don't always do the wise thing. And it was the case that they weren't really clear in their own minds what their new plans were. This meant they relied on other people to put it into practice, lots of Quangos were set up. So under the Tories, education became a battlefield and the last people to be taken care of were the teachers and the children.

JZ: Do you think the Conservatives actually had an agenda then for breaking the morale of teachers? Did they see members of the profession as a left-wing mass who were going to rise up against them?

NdG: They've always seen teachers, and the NUT in particular, as a left-wing mass. I imagine they would have viewed us (NASUWT) as a mass, though not a left-wing mass. But, no, I don't think they arrived in power in 1979 with the express wish to do to teachers what they eventually did to them. I'm not sure they even had an agenda to dismantle the unions, but they definitely wanted to impose discipline through monetarism and the NUM got involved in that long dispute. They played it very badly, I think.

There was a time when they could have got out with a lot of honour half way through. But he went on relentlessly to pursue the government did Arthur Scargill, and his open intent was to bring the government down through industrial action. So he set her up the way she wanted to be set up, because she was then able to say, certainly unions should dispute matters of pay and conditions, but they shouldn't be used as a battering ram against the government. He delivered his arse and it was kicked, and kicked rather severely.

She then moved on to conclude that after the NUM she could sort out the whole union movement. So I don't think Thatcher entered government in 1979 with that intention, but circumstances set up the opportunity to get excessively tough with the whole union movement and she took it. She was a very lucky Prime Minister. If it hadn't been for Galtieri in 1983 and the Falklands she probably would have lost office.

They'd had their monetarist experiment which had failed. They were getting into all sorts of trouble. They were unpopular. Then another opportunity in the shape of that idiot Galtieri came along and she saved herself again, made herself very

A Class Act

popular. Also Labour was in deep trouble by then and drifted away almost into oblivion.

JZ: In terms of new Labour, then, where we are now - there have been lots of positive noises about education, lots of pledges and some money. But it still seems that much of government rhetoric is as negative as it ever was under the Tories. Tony Blair said of the state sector - 'There's too much expectation of mediocrity' - do you think that the rhetoric is still quite negative?

NdG: There's a deliberate two-track message coming out from the government. They've taken a conscious decision about this. They will both praise teachers and criticise them and underline the need for radical reform to raise standards. So it's like a stick and carrot approach. And that's quite a deliberate decision they've taken.

I asked Labour people about this and someone very close to number 10 eventually told me that "that is the message they've decided to convey". They think this will make them populist - that it's the right message for the public: teachers need to be kicked and yet they give the right message to the profession too, saying they want to praise us.

So you get Tony Blair in New York saying that we [teachers] are a vested interest to be confronted and in Blackpool we hear Blunkett describe us as the nation's most precious national asset. This is deliberate ambivalence. Teachers on the whole are very disappointed. They expect a lot better from new Labour.

JZ: Are you personally disillusioned?

NdG: Yes - well, it depends what you mean by disillusioned. I'm saddened but not surprised, because you only had to pay attention to what they were saying when Blair took over the leadership to realise that there were huge problems in store for us. We were complaining about the workload for teachers under the Tories, but you could see that even in opposition new Labour were lining up a whole host of new initiatives that would just add to that workload. Some of these changes might be good ones in principle, but any change is dodgy these days because the profession is so fatigued by constant reform. Even good changes, at this time, present their own problems.

A Class Act

DP: Given that you've voiced some degree of dissatisfaction with new Labour what do you make of the proposed Superteacher initiative and Performance Related Pay?

NdG: The advanced skills teachers idea is good in principle - reward good practice. I think that's the germ of a good idea. Keep those good teachers in the classroom. The status and pay should remain in the classroom. But the idea has been aborted in practice because even now these teachers who have been identified as having excellent skills spend more and more time out of the classroom. They have to go to other schools and model what they do for others. So this is a heavy workload. It's a bad way to spread good practice. Have the teachers who wish to see good skills come to the selected teacher, not the other way round.

And your point about PRP. Actually, Labour are not proposing a simple PRP model. It's a combination of appraisal-related pay, and some performance related bonuses. Any extra money you get might be linked not just to what you do, but what your pupils do as well. So it's a mixed picture.

The NASUWT is happy with appraisal related pay - we think that's quite fair. In fact we've long advocated that. Appraisal related pay focuses on the input - what teachers put into the job of teaching and learning. It doesn't focus on the exam results of children or SATs results. Since they'll always be variance between different classes and over time it seems to me fairer to use this system that PRP.

JZ: Surely, even using this model, the notion of extra pay for some members of staff is basically divisive? One of the strengths of effective teaching in schools is being part of a team. Won't that be eroded away by appraisal or performance related pay?

NdG: It's no more divisive than the current system. It's quite fallacious to say that teachers are currently all paid the same because they're not. About half are on point 9 and that number is shrinking all the time. So the opportunity to reach a decent point on the pay scale may not be there for teachers in the way it was up until now. Budgets are shrinking and money is being used for other purposes. We are all paid the same only in the sense that we're all at different points along the same spine, with regard to responsibilities some of which are genuine, some of which are spurious.

A Class Act

So there is some differentiation to be made, but the NASUWT would be against that differentiation being too fine, too multi-layered. You could then find yourself getting involved in nonsense judgements about small differences, petty differences, and I think they would be very divisive.

We should be distinguishing between the high-flyers, most teachers would fall in the average. And then you do get the bottom ten per cent who perhaps shouldn't be there. They're not performing, or maybe they're under performing and that wouldn't be a bad message to give. You know, you're not up for the sack immediately, but you're not a very inspiring teacher, you're not going to have a very promising career. You've had a few years at it, you've not improved - you can stay at 20,000 but that's going to be your lot. And if that message is given it's not necessarily a bad message to give. In some ways it's quite essential if you're going to raise standards.

JZ: Do you really think the figure is as high as 10% of uninspiring teachers or are you just pulling a figure out of the air?

NdG: I'm just using it as an example. It could be 5% or Chris Woodhead's 4% - it's neither here nor there. It's useless to speculate about figures like that in public. But if you're going to get - as we would like - an extremely competent classroom teacher being paid 30,000 by the time they're 30 years old, which is a modest professional salary, and the teacher pay bill is enormous, then it's unrealistic to expect everyone to qualify for that 30,000. We just wouldn't get the money.

DP: Can we move on to ask you some questions specifically about the role of unions within teaching. What's your position on this idea of the teaching unions merging to act as a stronger force?

NdG: I disagree with the assumption that merging would make the unions a stronger force. We'd permanently ensconce the majority against ever taking action against anything. Sometimes a time comes when an employee needs to stand up to their employer - even where that employer is a government - and say 'no this is unreasonable.' Now that is a clear trade union commitment. By being in a trade union you declare your willingness to participate in the process of standing up for your rights and the rights of other members, should the issue arise.

A Class Act

Now most teachers would rather not take action - and the extreme view of the PAT, that it is never acceptable to do so, is one I respect - but I have a different judgement. If you merged all unions - including the Headteacher's union, the ATL and the soft underbelly of the NUT, which is mostly based in the primary sector - then you'd have a union, the majority of whose members would never be in favour of taking action. You'd render teaching unions less effective. The quality of the union is more important than the number.

JZ: What about the criticisms that teachers level at unions - that they have failed to win the hearts and minds of the public with regard to teaching issues generally, that they haven't been proactive enough, but rather reactive to government legislation and initiatives?

NdG: It is something we've tried to do, but it proves impossible to get coverage of good positive news. You come out with a positive statement the media won't run with it. They've got to get the controversy. So teachers who say we've failed are right, to an extent, but they shouldn't think we haven't tried. Local newspapers are different. There the emphasis on community permits the odd piece of good news some space in amongst the bad. But at national level it's impossible.

DP: So do you think that some sections of the press purposely vilify teachers?

NdG: Yes! And purposely vilify trade unions. Not just teaching unions. Partly because of the experience of Fleet Street and all the malpractice and therefore they're violently opposed to unions. They're vitriolic in their opposition because a strong union will ensure the cake is divided more evenly.

JZ: A very big issue for everyone in the profession is Ofsted. Do you think that 1) the present system is damaging to schools and 2) that Chris Woodhead as HMCI has purposely caused unnecessary tensions and difficulties for teachers?

NdG: Undoubtedly the Ofsted system is damaging to teachers. The facts speak for themselves. Thousands upon thousands of teachers complain. There's the stress the sickness...and an enormous amount of anti-climax even after they've had a good report. That's the strange thing about it. The way I like to think about it is to compare the performance of schools, the outputs if you like, across Northern Ireland, Wales and Scotland.

A Class Act

Take Wales for example. Wales is a more impoverished area, both in rural and urban settings, than England. Yet in GCSE results 46% of pupils obtained grades A to C. In England the figure was 46.3%. Now Wales doesn't have the heavy handed inspection system we have here under Ofsted, but their results are pretty similar. So what is Ofsted adding? Not much it would seem. In fact, the additional effect of Ofsted in the long term will probably be debilitating, because if it does one thing it's to encourage good teachers to leave the profession.

DP: Is it not ultimately a question of professional autonomy? I mean if you look at Switzerland for example, standards are high in terms of output. Teachers are paid well, and they have a massive amount of professional autonomy. What came first there? Probably the autonomy, because you won't get the best people applying if they're made to feel inadequate by an intrusive, over elaborate system of inspection.

NdG: I would criticise Ofsted and in fact all the initiatives over recent years because they have concentrated on structures and systems when they should have addressed the issue of 'how do we get good people in to the profession?' If you can crack that - and it may cost money - so much of the other stuff would take care of itself.

One of the reasons teachers have little professional autonomy is that over a period of years their confidence has been eroded from every quarter. Even twenty years ago we can't kid ourselves that teachers had professional autonomy. I mean they did, but only if they were happy to stay where they were.

Promotion opportunities back then were determined by how well you jumped to the tune of the trendy teaching inspectors who peddled a brand of teaching which sounded great on paper, but which was impossible to put into practice without chaos being the result. I was London Secretary in the early to mid-seventies and I can remember seeing teacher autonomy in the classroom being abused really. I mean teachers had completely lost control.

It's ironic because back then I would tell the then Education Secretary, Margaret Thatcher, that there were thousands of failing schools only to be told to go away and stop exaggerating. So I'm bloody sick of Labour politicians lecturing me on failing schools. Now the pendulum has swung back to didacticism. But there's still

A Class Act

an agenda being dictated.

JZ: If we could come back to Chris Woodhead for a moment. He is obviously a kind of hate-figure within the profession. Is that justifiable? Has he gone out of his way to cause unnecessary problems?

NdG: I think to some extent he's been demonised by teachers and to a certain extent he bought it on himself. I think two things he did wrong were, firstly, to leak his own findings on the effects of class size and his statement that class size wasn't the most important thing. And in one sense of course it isn't. A good teacher in a big class is probably going to do a better job than a bad teacher in a small class. Now he misinterpreted the findings - I assume deliberately - and when the report finally came out it said that for a large number of pupils class size was important. So he undermined his own report and that surprised and angered a lot of teachers. Secondly, that figure he plucked out of the sky - that there are 15,000 incompetent teachers.

JZ: Well, when we interviewed him, he said that Ofsted would be publishing statistical evidence to back up the initial figure. And those figures, he says will prove that there are 15,000 failing teachers.

NdG: Well it's interesting that he's now got figures to support his contention of three years ago. It should have been the other way round. Even then, it's only 4 per cent. I mean to turn that round, we can say that 96% of teachers are doing a satisfactory or good job. But he takes a different starting point. Yes, 4% is a problem. But let's put that in context. The media feeds off him and he feeds off the media.

Essentially, the problem with Ofsted is that it is a very public way of managing people, one that ultimately lowers the amount of respect which teachers are accorded. You can't expect parents, and pupils for that matter, to have faith in teachers if they are constantly undermined in public. I can't think of a single profession or indeed any other sphere of working life where the workers receive such a public dressing down.

DP: What do you make of the notion of primary schools being 'community hubs,' the basic contention being that the primary school premises would be used by the

A Class Act

local people as a centre for a number of activities. The ultimate contention being that the primary school could offer a 'range of services' beyond those of education. There has been talk of Headteachers 'diversifying' - all very free-market.

NdG: It depends on whether they're prepared to properly resource it. I mean turning a school into a facility which meets a wide range of community needs is very laudable but there are issues about job descriptions, demarcation of responsibilities...it would be nice if schools could do that. But you then have to be sure that whatever use the building has been put to in the evening, weekend, whatever, that it is ready in every sense to be used for the purpose for which it was intended the next morning.

You can't have the atmosphere of 'leisure' seeping into the whole notion of teaching and learning. That wouldn't be good.

JZ: You have often had a high media profile when you've made a stand for teachers' rights over the years. Often it has seemed to be you alone. Is that lonely? Do you feel you're banging your head against a brick wall?

NdG: I don't feel lonely. I get good support. One always likes to be positive. But one can't invent that. I know Blunkett and others accuse me of being negative too much of the time. But I don't look for negativity. I judge life on its merits, as I've told him to his face on more than one occasion. I'm not going to cease making the comments I made to the Tories simply because a new Education Secretary is in office, when all of the same problems persist.

JZ: Finishing off then - are you optimistic about the future for teachers under the current government?

NdG: It's better now than under the Tories. There are many good things Labour are doing and others that they're trying to do. I recognise that as cause for optimism. However, they don't have the kudos they might have. For example, announcing 1.3 billion for education a year ago was great, except half way through that statement Blunkett adds that not one penny of this must go towards teachers pay. So at a stroke, all the uplift in morale which should have flowed from that statement was wiped out.

A Class Act

The failure of Labour is to not yet make the changes that will really make a difference to do good for real people doing real jobs, and that, of course, includes teachers. But the potential is there for a lot more good. You have to travel in hope, and the NASUWT will try to make those good things happen.

A Class Act

17. *The Great Escape.*

Leave If you must but don't close the door.

Most Commonly Cited Reasons For leaving The Teaching Profession.

I don't like my Headteacher.
I don't like the staff.
I have no time for children.
I want a larger car.
I don't want to ever see a take-away sum again.
The government makes me feel useless.
I want to travel.
I feel too institutionalised.
It's boring.
I want to wear shoulder pads to work.
I'm tired of packet soup.
I want to save money.
I don't want to talk to anyone during the working day.
I want my own office.
I don't want to be answerable to any one.
I don't feel valued by society.
I want to work with animals.
I've given everything I've got.
I want to work for Her Majesty's Prison service.
There have been too many changes to the job.
I forged my teaching qualifications.
I want to wear designer clothes.
I want to be greedy for a change.
I don't like the smell of disinfectant.
I've never got the maths right in the back of my register.
I can't face another Ofsted inspection.
I don't want to ever sit in a staff meeting again.
My classroom is always too hot or too cold.
I don't believe in education.
I want to work in the double-glazing industry.

A Class Act

Teaching, like that other fine and ancient institution, marriage, can sometimes run into problems. You are practised at your art. You have a stable and successful routine which onlookers admire, and which you yourself can appreciate as a mark of professionalism and excellence. Your year is structured by the waxing and waning of an academic moon. The first month of your calendar is not January, but September. The last is not December, but July. You have evolved into a different species almost. A being whose life is deeply embedded in the conventions set down in times of yore by the elders in the teaching tribe. You have completed a rite of passage not open to the majority, and you know that this second socialisation is over. You are inside the system. You have made it. Well done.

Now what?

That's a good question, because supreme competence often comes in a package deal with boredom. You are restless. Yes, climbing the teaching mountain was a challenge, but now that you've reached the summit...well, you don't want to come down exactly, you don't want to retrace each step you made in the ascent. But you do want to do something more than admire the tremendous view. It's often at this juncture, while you're looking around at the never ending horizon, that you realise what should have been so obvious all along: you can jump.

The free-fall out of teaching offers all the exhilaration of the route into the profession, only at ten times the speed. Once you've considered jumping it's only a matter of time before you start looking into the least bumpy routes down the rockface. You begin to make some enquiries, and start to map out a potential flight path into the fertile valley of opportunity.

As you traverse the highways and byways of this land, you glance enviously in the windows of temping agencies (which, incidentally, you think should be renamed *tempting* agencies) and reel backwards at the pay and conditions for such posts as 'credit controller', 'stock engineer', and 'genetic mutator'. By exploring what is *out there* you start to feel a tug that pulls you towards the possibilities of completely different working cultures altogether. Why shouldn't I work in a glamorous environment for once, you reason, where there is a fresh croissant machine and I can carry a gold company credit card?

You begin to examine a whole swathe of adverts, in the hope that someone is searching for your talents. Creative and media job sections are raked through in the hope of finding an inroad into television, or perhaps even the burgeoning British film industry. Perhaps you could become a director or maybe a dolly-grip. You

A Class Act

spend all of your lunchtimes hunting for a quiet room to make that call to a ten-a-penny recruitment firm who play hard to get when you attempt to sell your soul to their media sales pitch.

The salaries accompanying Information and Communication Technology posts sets the cash tills in your mind frantically opening and closing, but the vision disappears in a cloud of missed promise, as you realise you possess no relevant qualifications and have been taught all you know about the class computer by a seven year-old.

Perhaps the charity sector would welcome your skills, as more adverts are chanced upon. But the starting salaries are below even yours, and with no experience, the bottom is the only place for you to begin. It seems so hopeless. You are qualified to teach, and that is surely all you will ever do. You stop off on the way home from school and place all of the exciting sounding adverts into a recycling bin.

All this pondering you are doing, all of the standing on the edge of the precipice is complicated by the fact that for lots of genuine reasons, you hold a deep abiding love for teaching. You believe in it. Of all the possible jobs, when all is going smoothly, nothing can beat it for satisfaction and altruistic worth. It is at this juncture that you realise free-fall might be a little too radical. You put to one side the application forms for 'Managing Director of offshore bank' and 'Head of Personnel at medium-sized pharmaceutical company.' Maybe things are looking up.

You begin to entertain the notion of strapping a parachute to your back.

You start to carry a small jotting pad in a fold of your coat, and on Fridays when the staffroom is quiet, you furtively scribble down a series of useful contacts and addresses as found within the pages of the *Times Educational Supplement*. These are all found towards the back of the appointments section, and none of them are actually based in schools. They are for 'teaching-related' posts.

The beautiful thing about the education profession is the way in which a whole string of satellite jobs have evolved, which can satisfy your hunger for change whilst simultaneously keeping you grounded in schools and the business of learning. Jobs such as Educational Psychologist, Museum Education Officer, Educational Researcher, Education Media Planner, Educational Publisher all proliferate in a process of natural selection. Your desire to escape the classroom, either temporarily or forever, is aided and abetted by the exponential growth of such

A Class Act

jobs. Teachers can transform themselves into educationalists.

So what exactly are educationalists and what is their role in society? An educationalist can be broadly defined as one who works within the sphere of education, but doesn't spend too much time in the classroom. There are exceptions to this, with some educationalists barely visiting their offices, choosing instead to complete surveys and questionnaires in classes and school corridors.

For many educationalists however, the real business of their day takes place at a desk, which probably has set upon it an Apple Macintosh complete with 32x CD Rom, 56K Modem with internet connection, Einstein Screen Saver and a Wallace and Gromet mouse mat (they like to maintain an air of impish dissent). Educationalists read journals and the TES. They write for journals and the TES. They possibly even subscribe to journals and the TES, although this is extremely unlikely, as no educationalist worth their salt pays for publications which their funding father or mother institution should rightfully buy.

A selection of the articles in educational publications are of real value, although it is never certain how many people ever read them. But, there is a trend within these outlets, to print some incredibly obscure pieces of opinion and research. Some of the more offbeat entries in recent years include:

The image of the thimble in Shakespeare's tragedies. How does it affect the teaching of Religious Education?

The Balsa Wood Paradox. Is carpentry the new drama?

Fountain pen versus biro. Does smudging affect literacy attainment?

Disney cartoons as a metaphor for social realism. Is the Lion King a communist parable?

Climbing frame games in infant playgrounds. A comparative analysis with the social behaviours of scampi.

Leading in darkness. Can the literacy hour be taught whilst blindfolded?

Many of those who have made the move into the educationalist world, do find that they now have the time and energy to argue about education policy and practice. They find that being removed from a classroom environment gives them the

A Class Act

freedom to hold an opinion. No longer shackled to a punishing timetable and a classroom of warring tribes, they start to feel a passion and commitment towards education which at times was lacking during the years of rolling through the school gates, cradling a Pisa-like tower of unmarked maths books. They enjoy their visits to school in the name of research, content to look on knowingly as a hoarse teacher attempts to control a crescendo of noise.

Many who do leave the class for the world of educationalism, continue to make valuable contributions to the lives' of schools and teachers, sometimes lobbying on their behalf through research papers, meetings with ministers or press conferences. Others however are content to enter their new office and firmly shut the door, making it impossible to hear even the distant muffled sounds of a nearby school on lunch break.

Some teachers make the jump and land in the rather busy offices of an educational publishing house. At the outset, the ex-teacher sets out to commission the perfect literacy scheme that will teach the world to read. Perhaps their name could be attached to this fantastic, universal tool, thereby achieving their immortality. Perhaps they could edit it, or even re-write some of the material. Such ambition is soon quashed by the flurry of dog-eared manuscripts about a duck on a search for self-esteem. These need to be returned in brown envelopes with a standard rejection letter. As the weeks roll by, the in-tray fills with more examples of parables featuring furry animals and household furniture, but no literacy schemes arrive.

So do you fancy it? Do the worlds of research or publishing attract you? Do you want to attempt the leap for yourself? Before you decide to do anything, it's worth being reminded that many who float down into the lush greenness of the money fields, soon tire of the trinkets they find there. As they toss aside another expensive bauble secured by the elasticity of their expense account, they may just find themselves looking up at the wondrous peak of knowledge, snow-capped and magisterial, rising high up above the plain, and see it afresh as if with new eyes.

A new form of gnawing inadequacy is triggered within them. Now they feel they have 'sold out', that they've opted for a set of values which set at nought the very principles they cherished as a teacher. What about knowledge for knowledge's sake? What about the awe and wonder one can feel at making sense of the world around you? What about the chance to play football every day, with kids half your size, whom you can easily push off the ball to score blistering goals from thirty yards out? More than this, anyone who has jumped badly misses the well-earned

A Class Act

and much appreciated long holidays, which were always one of the big attractions of teaching. Faced with twenty five days holiday (count them, just twenty five. In numerals it looks like this: 25) those in the valley soon start to question their decision and yearn for the lengthy summer break, when they can pursue a life of freedom and relaxation.

Perhaps school life wasn't so bad after all. Maybe time out is only short-lived. Climbing back to the summit one previously flung oneself off is likely to leave a bitter taste in the mouth. It's true that returners are aided in their re-entry by already possessing the qualifications required. And all those years of experience will come in handy. One has, if you like, the equivalent of the Stannah stairlift as a useful bit of kit in any attempt to re-scale Everest. It's easier on the legs, but still takes ages.

If you *have* spent time out of the classroom, you're viewed with a fair amount of suspicion by other teachers when you return. You are tainted with the smear of twin scepticisms. Firstly, there is the premise, held by many, that you were damned lucky to get out in the first place, and find yourself a job with your own phone, and in which you could call adults by their first names and not refer to them as 'Miss. Didbrook' or 'Mr. Ilsham.'

The other sceptical view is that having spent time amongst office workers, having had the free run of a photocopier in full knowledge that if it breaks down there's an *extension number* to ring, and having occasionally tasted the sweet fruits of a two-hour lunch break - how on earth will you be able to deal with the alternative universe that is your average school? It's like finding a child that's been suckled by wolves. Would you send it to Asda the same day you found it, with a shopping list and a fiver, and expect it to get very far?

Whether you're in teaching, out of teaching, thinking of leaving, or thinking of coming back to the fold, the lesson here is that you have choices. Many people assume that once you've qualified as a teacher then that is you labelled, packaged and on the shelf for life. That is not the truth. If you get into teaching and want to stay there then that's perfect. In spite of the supposed erosion of the 'job for life' in this country, many still stay and will stay in the profession for thirty or forty years.

If you do want to zig-zag in and out of the profession, then that's perfect too. The staggering thing about teaching is that it allows for this. It allows for the vagaries of the human condition and so engineers routes of escape knowing, as it does, that the journey is often circuitous and that every step you take will steadily bring you back to where you started.

A Class Act

18. Conclusion

What else can the 'Powers that be' place before us? In the recent past we've seen the following 'innovations'.

> Introduction of national curriculum.
> Re-introduction of national curriculum.
> Re-introduction of the re-introduced national curriculum.
> Creation of OFSTED.
> Introduction of SATS tasks and tests.
> Performance league tables.
> Naming and shaming of schools.
> Schools placed on *special measures.*
> Schools placed on *serious weaknesses.*
> Introduction of National Literacy Hour.
> Introduction of National Numeracy Hour.
> Proposed differentiated pay scales.

It is an unbelievable list, and pretty much goes to underpin one main point. Those in authority decided long ago that teachers were not performing well enough and that left to their own devices they would fail the nation's children. Therefore central governmental intervention was necessary, and if ministers and civil servants themselves couldn't go into classrooms to deliver lessons, then as sure as hell teachers would act as their mouthpieces, working in 'approved' ways, using 'established' methods and 'recommended practice'.

We are not saying that all of the changes have been bad. Far from it. Good has certainly come out of some of these policies, but bad has also accompanied any gains. And before anyone says 'just look at them, there they go again, the whinging, moaning, left-wing resistant to change idealogues who don't care about our childrens' education', we must remember that the overwhelming majority of teachers whilst questioning the validity of some of the more spurious facets of new policies, have actually been the ones to put them in place.

We have seen how the educational system has been pummelled from every quarter in recent times. We have seen how the collective psyche of teachers up and down the land has been bruised by the onslaught.

Yet, in all this mayhem teachers have continued to teach. And to teach well.

A Class Act

Government, Ofsted, parents even, should understand that teachers have persisted in circumstances many others would have balked at. In doing so they have met the policy makers and 'stakeholders' half-way. Perhaps it is time for other interested parties to start moving. Set out below are a few thoughts and recommendations which point to a way forward. These could be steps on a pathway out of the education quagmire. They could aid any 'interested parties' in reaching the juncture teachers arrived at some time ago.

1. Central Government.

The 'trust' and 'partnership' which are supposed to exist between the profession and government has to be a two-way process. We know where Tony Blair is coming from and we understand his obsession with hard-man tactics aimed at shoring up internal party support and stopping the obscene splits which used to divide his party. We know that when he talks of tough choices, he means that things aren't necessarily going to be easy, and just because it's Labour in power we can't expect a shorter working week and a hefty pay rise. WE KNOW!

But to continue with the rhetoric of the Conservatives in some areas is bitterly disappointing to many teachers. One of the points raised by both Doug McAvoy and Nigel de Gruchy concerned the 'twin-track' message emanating from government. Praise and shame. Laud and denigrate. The New Labour message as far as teachers are concerned is *"Tough on educational failure. Tough on the causes of educational failure."* This would be an acceptable mantra if the causes of educational failure were acknowledged to be a vast array of factors instead of simply 'poor teaching'.

Yes, there have been concessions, but all too often teachers are still solely being blamed for low exam results, schools at the bottom of league tables and declining standards of discipline.

A great opportunity exists for this government. There is still a sense of goodwill in staffrooms, but to build a bridge towards the teaching profession they must not only say they understand, but show they understand the complexity of education in today's society. The longer this government's term in office goes on, and the more drawn out its silence becomes over the issue of social deprivation and its effects on educational achievement, the more cynical teachers will become.

To acknowledge the role of disadvantage and poverty in the question of effective education is to take on a massive responsibility, and involves facing up to issues of taxation and redistribution of wealth. Maybe it's just easier to blame teachers than face the truth? It is no good every time a government minister panics about SATs

A Class Act

results, to launch a new shake up. David Blunkett stated that it would be a resigning issue for him if 80% of 11 year-olds didn't achieve level 4 in English by 2002. The figure for 1998 was 64%. It will be a remarkable feat if this target is reached. Of course, teachers want it to be reached, but the way to do this lies in factors outside schools as well as within classrooms.

The national literacy hour, just one in a long line of imposed initiatives that came down from on high, was introduced amidst a fanfare of publicity, but in reality is nothing more than a prescriptive guideline for teaching English in the way some teachers already taught it. It was fascinating to see on the training videos we were shown, hardly any children from diverse ethnic backgrounds and hardly any children with serious special educational behavioural needs.

The aims of the national literacy strategy are to be welcomed, but the process by which those aims are to be achieved is woefully unimaginative and too narrowly defined. It is a classic example of a pre-defined framework being imposed upon a widely varied set of individuals. Is it beyond the scope of the government's imagination to see that many groups will fall outside their framework?

Following the introduction of the numeracy hour in September 1999, we call for a moratorium on any other schemes, initiatives and directives which fundamentally alter the day to day workload of the average teacher. We have had so much new information to assimilate. We have changed so dramatically the way we work. Give us a period of time to adjust to change and to put everything into practice. There has been too much change for change's sake. How about a period of consolidation?

2. Ofsted.

Ofsted is all-pervasive within the teaching profession. And it shouldn't be. As a regulatory non-governmental organisation it singularly fails to effect positive change in our schools. One reason for this is the schools that needs Ofsted's help the most, are those whose circumstances and social contexts Ofsted continues to ignore.

There are many examples of schools which have been given glowing Ofsted reports, some of them may now be termed 'Beacon schools', but such schools were very probably already acknowledged by parents and the community as being excellent. It takes no skill or insight whatsoever to go to a good school and write a report that confirms exactly that. What takes talent, is to go to a school that is in

A Class Act

some respect 'failing' and leave some lasting impression on the staff, the children and the parents that change can follow.

Chris Woodhead talks often about the need to expect high standards even in the most socially deprived areas. He occasionally releases to the press a tale of one or two schools which achieve this success. What he has never properly and decently done, is make recommendations which could lead to the alleviation of the problems and hardships for schools in the most challenging situations. 'Special measures' and 'Serious weaknesses' have created stress and strain for those already working in the most difficult schools. This is inexcusable.

Once again a great opportunity is being missed here. Week in week out, teams of inspectors visit schools in a whole host of different circumstances and environments. What better chance could there be to establish, once and for all, the correlation between social disadvantage and educational attainment? But before Mr. Woodhead accuses us of dodging our responsibilities as teachers of children from all backgrounds, let us state quite clearly, that the level of teacher commitment can be sky-high, but still children will under achieve. What does this tell us? That perhaps other factors are involved here. Maybe it's time Mr. Woodhead took note of this. It doesn't take a rocket scientist to draw a parallel between disadvantage and effective education.

We tried to make this point to Mr. Woodhead when we interviewed him - that effective teachers could be rendered ineffective by a plethora of external factors. It was interesting to note that he accepted the point in terms of his own inspectors evidence being taken on board by teachers ie. Ofsted couldn't per se effect change in a school without the co-operation of teachers. Yet he wouldn't accept the same principle when applied to teaching ie. teachers couldn't effect change in a school without the co-operation of children and the wider community. Successful schools have this cooperation in spadefuls. Failing schools do not.

If Ofsted inspections are to have any validity at all, then they must accept that schools exist and work in partnership with the wider community, and that to some degree, their success or failure will depend upon the quality of that partnership. Therefore Ofsted reports should make recommendations not just to schools and teachers, but to parents and the local community. They should contain a far more substantive appraisal of the cultural and economic background of a school's catchment area.

This in no way shifts the responsibility of teaching away from teachers, but it does set their efforts in some kind of context and therefore would give any final report true meaning and validity. It is also very clear that some Ofsted teams are

A Class Act

often totally unprepared for, and unfamiliar with the types of schools they visit. It is all too hit and miss. Rural-based inspectors with knowledge of one-form entry village schools are not acceptable judges of inner-city multicultural educational establishments. There is not enough rigour in the training nor nearly enough thought in the deployment of inspectors.

Ofsted say they are accountable to government. Yet seeing Chris Woodhead cross-examined by a parliamentary Select Committee late at night on BBC2 is to see him dodge issues of importance, with the same lightfootedness he displays when faced with disgruntled teachers.

3. League Tables.

Skills skills skills. We are told that qualifications are everything, and that parents care more about exam results than anything else. We don't need academic studies to disprove this (although some have been carried out). No, ask nine out of ten parents what they really want from their child in school and they will say for their child to be happy, safe and to receive a good all-round education. Consecutive governments have been wrong in placing such a great emphasis on results and tables. For so long now, schools have been submitting results for inclusion in non value-added league tables. Yes, many boroughs do produce their own in-house value-added figures, but the results that reach the papers are still the raw results, which pitch a school in a deprived area against one in a wealthier suburb.

You can never underestimate how disheartening this whole process can be, however much teachers declare they have no interest in the league tables. Humans want to do well and are generally disappointed if they perform badly. If you know that you are a good teacher and people are constantly telling you so, neither of these factors will be of much comfort to you when your school comes bottom in the league table.

Sure, you have more children with special needs and English as an additional language in your borough, but you came bottom. You were last. You lost.

League tables are but one more example of how teaching has come to be perceived as a parody of what it once was. Now, the league tables would have us believe it's perfectly acceptable to ignore the thousand and one variables at work outside school and focus on the time spent in the classroom and nothing else. To say this gives you an insight into how well a school operates is tantamount to saying that your local newsagent should put its profits up for comparison with W.H. Smiths'.

A Class Act

Ofsted does produce 'Panda' reports and other similar documents that do compare the results of schools with similar backgrounds, but these documents hardly ever reach the public eye and it is almost as if they simply pay lip-service to the demands of teachers for value-added statistics. Non value-added league tables should be stopped. They offer no information of any worth whatsoever. What they cause is parental anxiety and teacher despondency for those in 'low-achieving' schools, and stress for those in 'high-achieving' schools who feel a great pressure to stay at the top. Children are also aware of them, and it would not be surprising if some were stigmatised by being at a 'sink' school.

Don't talk to us about competition with regard to education. Like health, education should be above the ebb and flow of market forces. Again we stress this doesn't mean to say aim low, and expect mediocrity. What we are saying, is you can only judge where a school has got to, and more importantly where it might get to in the future, if you understand where it started from.

4. Pay and Status.

Putting aside for one moment the burning issue of social deprivation and its effect on childrens' schooling, let us embrace the idea, however distasteful it might be, that there is a sizable proportion of teachers who aren't up to the job. If this notion were true, the most obvious way of improving the quality of the workforce would be to make the 'career package' more enticing. Do this with perhaps the added hurdle of tighter entrance qualifications and you up the quality of your applicants overnight. This is simplistic in the extreme but then so is much else espoused by the government at the present time, we might fairly assume it represents their thinking on this issue. However, instead of paying teachers more across the board, they have opted for what seems to be a strange and divisive solution.

The issue of pay thresholds and advanced skills teachers is one of the most patronising scams to be unleashed on us (and nurses too for that matter) and has been flung about without ever really being thought through. It is a political stunt aimed at proving the government is doing something to raise standards whilst making no efforts to raise morale and pride in the profession as whole.

Most teachers view it as little more than a joke, but the same was said about SATs and now they're here to stay. New pay proposals would create so much division and misery in the profession without making significant improvements in standards, that one wonders why the notion ever got off the drawing board.

A Class Act

Let's not beat around the bush, teachers deserve a pay-rise. *All* teachers, not just some. The profession is simply not rewarded enough for sheer hard work and commitment. If you want to judge the success of English schools as inspected by Ofsted, then compare the exam results and the SATs tests with Wales, with Scotland, for that matter with any comparable European country and you will find that by and large, it isn't a tale of woe and failure, but one of success. The problems English schools face in keeping up with the pace of change and the process of globalisation are faced by every school in every developed country around the world. Teachers are coping pretty well and should be recognised for their efforts.

The point nine pay ceiling has to be abolished. That is not to say that an infinite number of increments can be given out to all and sundry. It is merely to state boldly to those who wish to remain in the class; *we value you. We want you to stay, and here's the proof.* Yes it will cost any government dearly, but there is no way around it. If their promises about education are more than platitudes, they should be prepared to pay the price.

In terms of status, the most important development for teachers will be recognition of the fact that just like all other professionals, their effectiveness is directly linked to wider societal factors. No one would think of blaming a medical doctor for the smoking-related illnesses a patient may ask to have treated. People smoke. They do so today in the knowledge that it may harm their health. That's a reality. Doctors work within this reality. Similarly, teachers work with groups of people who for one reason or another find it difficult to accept the culture and values of the school. This too is a reality, and like doctors, teachers shouldn't be blamed for it.

Of course, teachers want to effect change and just as the medical profession puts across its message that smoking kills, so teachers must seek out ways to educate and raise awareness in communities who do not want to work in partnership with schools. But the facts of the matter should be acknowledged. Teachers operate in the real world, not in a vacuum, and the mass media need to be the first in a long line of organisations to get to grips with this.

****

So what of Nelson Rosario, Yolanda Monteith and their peers?

In the face of all the trials and tribulations heaped upon teachers in the modern

A Class Act

world, how have they fared in their quest to educate the nation's children and get a little job satisfaction into the bargain?

Nelson hasn't done too badly. He is now sufficiently familiar with the national curriculum to spend only two hours a night planning. He can spell all of the words on lists 1 and 2 of the national literacy strategy, but has some difficulties with list 3. He is currently teaching a year 5 class in a suburban school near Woking. Ambition led him to organise a county-wide table tennis championship which gave him ample opportunity to display his portfolio of trick shots. He insists that he would like to remain a class teacher, but if an opportunity for a Deputy Headship arose in a 'comfortable' school, he would consider it.

Yolanda is working in her mother's school as Deputy Head. This is both good and problematic. The positive aspects of this situation include working from home and whispering family secrets in staff meetings. The downside revolves around disputes over who should make the day's sandwiches. Yolanda's mum enjoys sending her daughter out on extra wet break duty just to remind her who's the boss.

And their peers? Many of the characters encountered between these pages have gone on to achieve great things in classrooms. Some have risen up the ranks and become very senior figures in the education world. Others have chosen to take the path out of the profession and haven't yet realised it's a cul-de-sac.

When they do, we look forward to welcoming them back.

And what of the Skegness Institute of Applied Mathematics? This was completely flattened by a butterfly flapping its wings in Banbury, thereby causing a freak storm in the north of England. This remarkable weather formation would have proved all of the Institute's propositions on chaos theory, but unfortunately all of their paperwork was destroyed.

****